LESS CLUTTER. LESS NOISE.

BEYOND BULLETINS, BROCHURES AND BAKE SALES

"...A MUST-KEEP-ON-THE-SHELF-CLOSE-TO-MY-DESK-FOREVER BOOK!"

"With a 360-degree view of the author and application of this book's content, I find myself in a unique position. As Kem's pastor, I've watched her integrate the values and principles espoused in this book throughout the fabric of Granger Community Church. This stuff isn't just theory. I know it really works. Kem has made this extraordinary material available to you. Use it up."

—Mark Beeson, Senior Pastor, Granger Community Church

"This book is a field guide for connecting with your community and transforming lives; it needs to be on every pastor's desk in America. Speaking from years of experience as an expert in corporate communications, Kem Meyer reminds us that the most effective communication tool is 'simplicity.' In today's multi-platform, complex media world, *Less Clutter. Less Noise.* is my reality check."

—Phil Cooke, filmmaker, media activist and author of *Branding Faith*

"The greatest message ought to be communicated in the most memorable ways. And, Kem Meyer will show you how to do it. This book is both inspirational and practical. A must read for those who care about communicating the message of Christ in the most compelling way possible."

—Mark Batterson, Lead Pastor, National Community Church and
Author of *In a Pit with a Lion on a Snowy Day*

"Practical, insightful, even breathtaking at times. If your communications are failing to communicate, this book is a fabulous place to start."

—Seth Godin, author of *Tribes*

"Those of us who communicate in local churches, seeking to inform and persuade, would be wise to pay attention to this book. Kem Meyer writes out of her own experience in a highly effective local church where she has learned what kinds of messages have the best shot at breaking through the clutter and compelling individuals to action. Thank you, Kem, for this extremely practical and helpful tool."

—Nancy Beach, Teaching Pastor, Willow Creek Community Church

"As a pastor, I spend a great deal of my time trying to figure out how to ensure that the message God has placed on my heart gets through the distractions of life into the hearts of the listener. Now, I have an amazing tool that can help me refine that art. Kem's book should be required reading, not just for pastors, but for anyone who needs to communicate with others. This is not only a must-read; it is a must-keep-on-the-shelf-close-to-my-desk-forever book! Buy it today!"

—Jonathan Falwell, Senior Pastor, Thomas Road Baptist Church

"As a leader, communication is key. And since we all communicate on a regular basis, pick up this book immediately. Whether web strategy, traditional mail, brochures, or social media, you'll learn from a proven and effective leader in Kem Meyer. After years of experience in both the corporate and church world, she understands what it takes to effectively get your message across. This book provides the lessons that will help you incorporate proven and practical communication practices into your organization."

—Brad Lomenick, Executive Director of Catalyst

"This book is a profound resource in the advancement of church communications. It will be a communication director's favorite and a hidden tool for savvy pastors."

—Richard Reising, author and president of Artistry Marketing

"Meyer takes a candid look at the stupid barriers that prevent progress and explains how to tear them down. By reading this book, evangelists in churches, non-profits, and businesses can learn to connect with the head, heart and gut of their customers and employees and then change the world."

—Guy Kawasaki, author of *Reality Check* and co-founder of Alltop.com

"Kem has written my kind of book, one that is entertaining, but also very practical with real 'meat' that can be quickly digested and used to fuel our self-improvement. She managed to cause me to smile, but also think and change."

—Dr. Al Long, author and professor at Indiana Wesleyan University

"Kem offers a much needed case for simplicity, clarity and communication strategy. It moves you beyond a barrage of information to a sharp, clear message, offering real and practical advice you can apply to your own situation."

—Steve Smith, author, speaker, creative architect and founder of Ordered List

LESS CLUTTER. LESS NOISE.
BEYOND BULLETINS, BROCHURES AND BAKE SALES

kem meyer

PRESS

Less Clutter. Less Noise.

Kem Meyer

ISBN-13: 9780979589959

ISBN-10: 0979589959

Library of Congress Control Number: 2009900352

This book is manufactured in the United States of America.

Thirty:One Press
13680 N. Duncan Dr.
Camby, IN 46113
(317) 347-1051
thirtyonepress.com

Editor: Susan Andres
Cover and Interior Design: Lisa DeSelm
Author Photo: Daley Hake

CONTENTS

INTRODUCTION

Life is hard and people are bombarded, used, abused and skeptical. They live day to day in a stressed-out, over-committed, over-extended survival mode—whether they go to church or not. They simply don't have the margin for more, but they are looking for answers that will make a real difference in their lives.

The church should make it easy to find those answers. Most of the time, unfortunately, that is not what happens. Too often churches just add to the confusion.

Best Intentions with Disastrous Results
Scrambling to keep up and looking for ways to get their message heard, churches are creating more brochures, getting new logos, printing in four-color, advertising, emailing, building complex Web sites and writing clever content. By default, they try to communicate using methodologies that are all about "sending the right message."

Here's what happens. The people they are scrambling to reach do what they have to do to survive the onslaught. They shut down. Stop listening. Move on. Because more is not better.

Every organization, including the church, has to face a changing culture. Part of that requires us to get over ourselves and recognize that effective communication is really about "releasing the right response." The way to do it is by creating great experiences, a seamless message and a few smart systems. Sound complicated? It doesn't have to be!

Maybe This Is You
You are committed to helping people take steps in their spiritual lives. You may have even devoted your entire life to it. You know the local church can change hearts and lives, but you are struggling to make that connection with people in your community.

You really are trying to figure out how to get people to notice.

On the other hand, maybe you "get it." You have a few things in your toolbox that could break your church out of a rut, but you're having trouble getting buy-in from your staff, peers or leaders. Navigating through this change is frustrating and discouraging.

What You Need

Great communication strategies will make a noticeable difference, and many churches today are making efforts to get better at it. But even with an increased awareness of better "communications efforts," few understand the definition, and even fewer know how to manage it. Just as many people look to you for inspiration and practical answers, you are looking for practical answers, too.

You don't need to read an exhaustive textbook with heavy narrative and academic case studies to learn how to plan and run an effective communication strategy. What you do need is air. A fresh perspective. An encouraging nudge. A few "aha" moments. A simple example or two.

You Don't Know Me

Or even if you do know me, you might ask yourself as you're reading, "Who does she think she is?" That is a good question.

The beginning of my story is common. As a young adult, I was chasing everything that might compensate for the feelings on the inside I didn't know what to do with. Feelings of fear, insecurity, lack of purpose, loneliness, individuality—I had them all, even if I didn't recognize them for what they were.

Things in culture—things of beauty, art, excitement, fun, adventure—clearly captured my attention; they were not hard to find. I tried to fill the void with a career, more stuff and an active social life. On the outside, I was fulfilled and successful. I had it going on, but on the inside, I was empty. Without a foundation in Christ,

I lacked the filter to know which paths were empty facades and which were paths that would bring real life.

I was looking for inspiration and real answers that would make a difference in my life, but nothing about the church captured my attention. Even when I sought answers at the church, I could not find my next step. The church was like another world—one where I could not find a handle to hold onto. It didn't match anything I knew, so I left bombarded and confused and continued to chase the wrong things. My lasting impression of the church? It was for weak, out-of-touch people who just needed to "get a life."

Obviously, something happened along the way to change my mind. I was able to find real answers and see the tangible difference Jesus could play in my life. I was able to take steps and learn how God created me the way I am and that he has a plan for me.

Are you interested in how an organization can still capture someone's attention in the midst of all of the chaos and cultural momentum? Keep reading.

I have been part of Granger Community Church since 1991. I have worn every hat—skeptical guest, defensive attendee, lukewarm member, volunteer leader and committed staff member. I have watched and participated one step at a time as we've grown from an average weekend attendance of 400 to 6,000. Then, after 15 years of marketplace experience in corporate communications and Internet strategy, I left my corporate career and joined our staff team in 2002.

I started as an *outsider*, but now I am an *insider* who hasn't lost that "outsider's perspective." Whether you recognize it yet or not, your community has an outsider's perspective, too. People know they need "something more" but have stopped turning to the church for answers because its methods and language are clumsy and difficult. Sure, in times of crisis, ceremonial traditions or for an hour a week, the church is the place to be, but what about inspiration and direction for daily, normal life? Not so much.

So, for the past six years I've been teaching workshops, speaking at conferences and blogging about how to understand different worldviews and find ways to remove the barriers that keep people from connecting with Christ. In the process, I have broadened my knowledge base beyond one church. Over and over, I have listened to what leaders are saying and how they are dealing with pain and have found common issues that have brought me to this book. And, here we are.

Not Just for Churches
While this book was written from the vantage point of the local church, the principles speak loudly to schools, not-for-profits, small businesses or any organization struggling to get the word out to motivate their audience to action. With more than 450,000 churches and 78% of U.S. adult citizens identifying themselves as Christians, almost everyone in America has had some type of experience with the local church, directly and indirectly. And, although the U.S. has the lowest number of people claiming to have no religious beliefs, the uncertainty of religion in our country is one of the highest.

With studies showing around half of American adults leaving the faith tradition of their upbringing or abandoning religious affilia-tion altogether, what better organizational communication case study to learn from than the church in America?

How to Use This Book
A little background will help you digest what's next. My goal is to serve you with an easy, quick-reference, short course on incorpo-rating proven communication practices into your organization—regardless of size, style or location. This book does not follow the typical linear, A–Z outline. It caters to the short attention span (for my sake and yours). It is conversational. It bounces around. It uses

real stories and practical examples. You can read a few pages here and a few pages there. Relax, have fun and enjoy each bite-size serving. Each chapter will contain a new idea or story that encourages or challenges you to look at how you talk to people, create Web sites, print brochures, produce signage, make announcements, find resources, use technology, etc.

Although I will reference a variety of sources along the way, I have thought of you as I've developed the content in this book to deliver new insights from a real-life perspective. I realize this is crucial as you try to apply practical principles in a not-so-practical reality. Use the examples and stories in this book to promote team discussions in your world, bridge the gap and help leverage the power that already exists in your environment. I'm setting the stage now; the only way to reveal fresh observations is to put an end to preconceived notions. Every page is designed to provide you the context for reinvention.

Kym Meyer

part 1

ARE PEOPLE LETTING YOU IN OR SHUTTING YOU OUT?

Many times, conventional wisdom about communications and marketing is wrong. It mass markets, force-feeds and assumes people are just waiting to hear what you have to say. Are you unknowingly falling victim to believing five myths about getting the word out?

chapter 1
THE MYTH:
YOU ARE IN CONTROL

Every person has a unique framework of ideas and beliefs they use to interpret the world and interact with it—a *worldview*. A person's worldview holds in it his or her experiences, wishes, biases, values and assumptions. Good communication is not so much about sending the right message as it is releasing the right response. *The right message* assumes you and the other person will respond in the same way. A person's worldview shows up before you do, and that is the reality of the message you send. It's not what you say; it's what people hear. And, while you might not be able to control what people see or hear, you can do a better job trying to anticipate it.

IT'S A FRICKIN' ELEPHANT!

I heard a story about a grandpa helping his four-year-old grandson learn to read. The boy pointed to a picture in a zoo book and said, "Look, Grandpa! It's a frickin' elephant." The grandpa took a deep breath and asked, "What did you call it?"

His grandson repeated himself.

"It's a frickin' elephant, Grandpa! It says so on the picture!"

And, so it did. When the grandpa looked down at the picture, it read,

"A F R I C A N Elephant."

It's not what you say; it's what people hear. *

---

* Think you may have heard this before? It's the subtitle of a book by corporate and political consultant Frank Luntz—*Words that Work*.

ARE BIRDS TOO FEMININE?

Believe it or not, we processed this real question as a ministry team. The question arose when we were evaluating whether or not to use the image of a bird on our Web site. We have also discussed whether our baptism graphic resembled a female body part. Both of these conversations were totally serious and appropriate. It is important that you're willing to ask these types of questions before using graphics and images.

- Does this graphic support or compete with the intended experience for our audience?

- Does this visual help accomplish the desired objective or not?

- Does it have potential to attract or repel?

- Does it add to or take away credibility?

Do you remember seeing this image on billboard advertisements for Pepsi One[1] a few years ago?

What does this mean?[2]

When I saw it, I wondered why Pepsi was using a drop of blood to advertise their cola. The billboard would have made more sense for a hemophilia center or blood bank, but it did not make me want to drink Pepsi One, that's for sure. After a little research online, I discovered the experience they intended for their audience. The little blue guy is supposed to represent one calorie. The little red guy is supposed to represent taste. And, isn't that cute—they are coexisting happily together. See, you really can have it all.

Except, that is not the message I got driving down the road at 55 mph. They weren't in control of the message. **Sometimes, you need to evaluate a graphic's potential to take on a life of its own.**

In the end, we decided the particular bird image we were considering would send a more feminine message than we wanted. Although, we did all agree that a cardinal can put on a mean face.

IT TAKES TWO

Do we think about how what we say is going to affect others, or do we just think about what we have to say? I've heard David Armano, Experience Design guru, say it this way:

> **"Instead of asking *What are we trying to communicate?* which implies a one-way conversation...ask *How can we facilitate?*"**[3]

A friend of mine forwarded an example of someone's response to a form letter he received. It's a real-life demonstration of a message action and the reaction it triggered. I'm changing some names and details to protect the innocent, but here's the gist. A guy received a letter from a magazine worded exactly like this:

SUBSCRIPTION SUSPENDED

I'm disappointed.

You requested a subscription to *our magazine*, and I started that subscription for you in good faith. But so far, you haven't held up your end of the bargain.

I have no choice but to cancel your subscription unless we receive your payment in the next 10 days. Please mail it today.

This simple letter from the magazine seems harmless and normal enough, doesn't it? That is, until you see how it made the reader feel. The recipient tells the rest of the story in a candid response that gave voice to what many others feel but rarely communicate aloud.

Dear Editor,

When I was six, I regularly bullied my sister.

When I was 10, I stole candy from the Dollar Store, even though I had the money to pay for it.

When I was 14, I broke my mother's heart by yelling at her to leave my baseball game because she was embarrassing me.

When I was 19, I regularly pilfered wads of toilet paper and Ziploc bags of hand soap from my place of employment.

I'm impatient with my kids. I'm selfish. I judge people harshly. I'm not as kind to strangers as I should be. I don't like animals. I take the miracle of my life for granted. I'm ungrateful. I'm obscene. I make absurd banalities into "issues" just so I don't feel boring. I once instigated a fight with my wife over green beans.

I am not as good as I could be. Of this, there can be no doubt.

Two months ago, I filled out a little card requesting a free copy of your magazine. After reading through it, I chose not to subscribe. Was I disappointed in the quality of the writing? Did I find it over-priced? Did I get busy with giving birth and raising an infant and forget all about it?

You didn't ask, and I am disappointed. Had I received a kinder message from you such as "I'm sorry you chose not to subscribe to our magazine. Please keep us in mind in the future. Please have a nice day." I would have considered sending a check for $12.95.

Please take me off your mailing list. I have enough to feel ashamed of in my life without more guilt trips from you.

I wonder what candid feedback we'd hear about letters we send out if we asked. How often do I draft my correspondence, seemingly harmless enough, without concentrated consideration as to how it makes the recipient feel? Do I test my words against the desired objective I'm trying to accomplish?

I appreciate the insight I gained from this honest response to a thoughtless form letter. When I'm able to get insight such as this, it helps me anticipate responses. Only then am I able to communicate in a way that opens doors instead of closing them.

WAIT FOR IT

I don't necessarily like surprises, but I do love the unexpected. I love it when someone breaks away from the norm to introduce a fresh approach. When I can't predict what's going to happen, I'm left going "Huh. How about that?" I like it when that happens.

A close friend of mine attended our weekend service and sat down behind a family with a teenage boy playing his Game Boy. As the service started, my friend was irritated that the boy continued to play his game. The longer the service went on and the boy kept playing, the more agitated he became. It was on mute but still distracting and unnerving in the middle of the service. He was just about ready to lean forward to ask the boy to put the game away when something caused him to stop. He waited a few minutes, leaned forward, tapped the boy on the shoulder, and said,

> "I've got the guide with all the moves to beat that game if you want it."

Huh. How about that?

What my friend did not know was that the teenage boy in front of him was autistic. He also did not know that the family hadn't been able to attend church for years because of their son's inability to sit still. They had been asked to leave public places numerous times because of the boy's erratic behavior. When the boy's parents saw my friend lean forward and tap their son on the shoulder, they immediately assumed the worst. "Here we go again."

But, they experienced an unpredictable comment, wouldn't you agree? It even took my friend by surprise, and he's the one who said it! I am so glad he kept his heart open and was slow to speak.

It's easy to judge people who are not like me. It's easy to dismiss people who act in a way I just don't understand. It's also easy to slip into this complacent mode where I think "I've got it all figured out." Then, my unsolicited sermons into those people's lives are destructive because I don't have all the information. I end up keeping score based on my own personal worldview—a worldview that lacks important context outside of my individual walk.

> **"Your life bears a message, a message of hope and redemption. But, before people in your world encounter your message, they encounter you."**[4]

Ouch.

Rob Wegner, our pastor of Life Mission, communicated this topic last year when he spoke at the Innovate conference. He talked about the two parts to the great commission. Part one is "How do we get people into the church?" Part two is "How do we get the church into the community?" He said the only way to do that is to make some "missional moves." In other words, move on mission. Rob's leadership has mobilized hundreds of people in our church to move on mission to make an impact on thousands of lives in the global community.

But, do you know what is just as honorable? Rob is the friend I talk about in this story. He does not forget that Jesus gives us multiple spheres of community influence. Rob is responsible with every one—be it with people in India or the boy sitting in the seat in front of him playing with his Game Boy during church.

It is healthy to renew our perspective. Because what we are familiar with, we cease to see.

DO YOU HAVE ACCURATE INFORMATION?

I was driving home from visiting my sister in Cincinnati, and as I passed a truck, the driver honked. My first instinct was "Hey, I'm in my lane...what are you honking at?"

I drive a little farther, and another truck honks as I pass. This time, I wonder if I have a flat tire or something is sticking out of one of my doors. I check my gauges. They all look good. I continue driving.

Another truck honks at me! This time, I confess, my mind goes here... "Well, I *am* aging gracefully. I guess I shouldn't be surprised I can still get the attention of a trucker. I should be flattered."

As I drive for the next thirty miles, four out of five truckers honk as I go by. As deluded as I may have been in the previous paragraph, I am not an idiot. Something is wrong, and I know it. I'm not *all that* and even if I were, there aren't that many cavemen on the road at once.

It is only then I catch a glimpse of my kids, Emmi and Easton, in my rear view mirror pulling an imaginary chain in the air as we passed another truck. Oh.

Turns out all of those cavemen on the road weren't honking at me; they were engaging in a childhood game* that has been passed through the generations. They were just playing along and honking their horns in response to my kids' hand motions.

Awwww. In an instant, they went from perverts to participants. From cavemen to child advocates.

See how easy it is to mistake personal perceptions with the greater reality? Or, am I the only one who does that?

---

* Children act out pulling an imaginary rope as every truck passes on the highway to make the big ol' semi honk. If the trucker honks, kids laugh and squeal. If the trucker drives on by with no honk or wave, then kids are sad until the next try.

YOU'RE NOT THE BOSS OF ME

I read a post on Google's corporate blog last year about how to use the word "google" properly and improperly in a sentence. Their *helpful tips* were an attempt to rebound from the word "Google" slipping from trademarked status into common usage. It was frustrating to read. The short story? Google was slapping our wrist for how we use their corporate name in our conversations. Apparently, their huge success and influence on pop culture had distressed their trademark lawyers, and they wanted us to know what we could do about it.

Yougottabekiddingme.

TO: GOOGLE   **FROM:** KEM

Oh, Google. Please don't go there...you will lose tons of street credibility and trust if you continue to make this an issue.

Somebody in marketing or legal is forgetting the attributes that have gotten you to where you are today...it's not all about your technology...it's about the stuff you give away for free...it's about how you let us do what we want to do without prescribing a path...it's about how you're pushing the envelope, not fitting the mold.

All this time, Google, you made us think it was **all about us**...and we loved you for it. We changed the way we talk, surf and build sites because of you. But, this sounds like it's **all about you**...and now my radar is up.

Are you just like all the other guys? I thought you were different.

In some instances, **a message might be important to your INTERNAL corporate audience but completely absurd for your EXTERNAL audience. Do you know the difference?**

Sigh. Now I'm wondering if I can be sued for being Googlicious.*

---

* Googlicious—adjective describing a Web site that ranks high on Google searches.

NOBODY LIKES TO PLAY WITH A CONTROL FREAK

I thought this was a joke, but then I went to the LEGO corporate site to see for myself. Here's the screenshot from my computer:

Thankfully, Lego has updated their home page[5] since I first captured this.

The folks at Lego have missed the point. Who seriously approved this "IMPORTANT NOTICE" to their customers? What message are they trying to send? **Who are they trying to serve—the customer or themselves?** I can just imagine the conversation in the boardroom:

> So, hey everybody! Our LEGO bricks are a household name. Everybody talks about them. Everybody plays with them. Everybody buys them for their kids and builds cities with them. But, you know what, people? We're failing at our job because nobody's saying it right! They call them LEGOs instead of LEGO toys or LEGO bricks. The nerve. Our customers are getting it all wrong, and we've got to set them

straight. We need an important notice on our Web site. Quick, before one more customer gets it wrong!

Surely, they were hacked. Tell me it isn't true.

Note to self: Don't be a control freak with church communications.

THINK IT OVER

Busting the myth—you are in control.

- ☐ Where do I think I have all the answers? Are there places I need to go, people I need to see or experiences I need to feel to keep my mind and heart open? Do I surround myself with "yes" people? Am I avoiding the hard work of differing perspectives, seeking only input and answers that support my thoughts and views?

- ☐ How can I stop myself from trying to push my audience to a decision or to my point of view? Are there incremental steps I could lay as groundwork to pull people into the content I have to offer?

- ☐ Where am I applying my worldview on others? Am I inadvertently putting out a message to meet my needs rather than thinking through the worldview of my guests? How can I permeate "give them the benefit of the doubt for a moment" into my everyday thinking?

- ☐ In what ways could my message be misunderstood based on the worldview of my audience? What could help prevent that? Has there been an instance where I failed in communication by assuming the wrong thing?

- ☐ Where am I engaged in corporate self-talk? Are there formal or informal feedback mechanisms in place to help identify communication misses?

- ☐ What can I do to help all of our external communication spring from the same platform?

chapter 2

THE MYTH: THE MORE CHOICES, THE BETTER

A Sunday edition of the *New York Times* carries more information than the average nineteenth century citizen accessed his entire life.[1] Information used to be as rare and precious as gold; now, it is so inexpensive and plentiful that most of it ends up being overlooked, ignored or tossed like garbage. As of February 2007, there were over 108 million distinct Web sites and increasing.[2] And, the barrage of data to which we are constantly exposed carries a cost—physically, mentally and financially—regardless of the generation. On average, consumers receive about 25 pieces of mail per week, more than half of it bulk mail.[3] People who live in today's world respond in one of three ways: they become overwhelmed and shut down, they labor over whether they're making the right decisions or they just ignore you and move on. *More* isn't what people are looking for; *relief* from the *pressure of more* is what they're looking for.

INFORMATION OBESITY

Information overload occurs when we receive more info than our brain can process. Even if it is good information, too much of a good thing just is not good anymore—it's bad. Whether you're an info addict or a Zen advocate, information overload affects us all.

Check out this excerpt from an article I read on ThinkSimpleNow.com about the cost of overfeeding the information appetite.

- **Productivity Loss.** In the face of too much information, we can easily get lost in the details. We waste time focusing on unimportant information and lose sight of our goal and purpose.

- **Mind Clutter.** The noise created by media and other sources of information clutters our minds and takes away from our inner peace.

- **Lack of Time.** Rich or poor, young or old, we all have the same limited amount of time in a day. And instead of spending a good chunk of my day filtering through incoming information, I'd rather spend the energy on bringing more enjoyment and fulfillment into my life.

- **Lack of Personal Reflection.** I find that if I am constantly consuming information, then I forget to connect with myself (and others). I realize that valuable personal reflection comes when we create a "space" for it in our lives. If there is always noise, then we won't have the mental capacity to reflect within.

- **Stress & Anxiety.** Information inflow creates the illusion that we have more tasks to fill our lives than we have time for. Often, we might suddenly feel nervous without understanding why. Every piece of information carries with it energy which demands our time. Even if we consciously ignore it, a part of us saw that data and recorded it within our subconscious.[4]

Life is overwhelming enough as it is. Your church or organization shouldn't be piling more on top of an already mounting problem, especially when people are looking for answers that will make a difference. If you want to be a credible source for those answers, here are ways you should be looking to help reduce that load.

- **Stick to the facts.** Don't over-sell, over-explain or over-control. Just provide the information someone needs to self-sort and self-decide. People don't need a page on the philosophy of each ministry, activity or event. They do need to know who it's for, what it is, when it happens and how to get there or sign up.

- **Stick to the point.** Start with the end in mind before you're about to do something. If you know the purpose behind your letter, brochure, meeting, etc., it makes it easier for you to stay on track and focused. Otherwise, it's hard to recognize your own excess. Do you want people to show up or respond? What are you asking them to do? If you can't answer that question easily, they won't be able to either.

- **Consider the crowd.** Does your announcement (bulletin or verbal) apply to everyone or just a handful of people? If it's not affecting the masses, it's just going to land like dead weight. Don't punish the crowd to keep a few people happy (even if they *are* the most vocal). Find a way to deliver your news in appropriate venues.

- **Don't intrude.** Unless they've asked for it, people welcome unsolicited emails as much as a door-to-door salesperson during family dinner. Respect personal space, and put information in a place easy for people to find when they want it.

According to a *Fast Company* magazine article, the Centers for Disease Control and Prevention states unequivocally that 80% of our medical expenditures are now stress-related.[5] Marketers have responded with superficial, tranquility promises: happiness in a perfume, peace in a lotion, focus in a drink, euphoria in a bubble bath, sex in a lip gloss, etc. **Our response should be less complex, more authentic and, ultimately, life-giving— it's as simple as dialing back the volume.**

POTATO CHIP DECISIONS

I heard author Gail MacDonald speak about a friend of hers who had moved overseas for mission work. She returned home to the United States after four years in the mission field. One of the first questions Gail asked her friend was "What's changed most in America the four years you've been away?"

The thing that changed the most in four years wasn't technology, health care or architecture. It was the potato chip aisle in the grocery store. When she left to go overseas, there were only a few types of chips to choose from, and now, there were hundreds of choices in multiple aisles.

Although that wasn't the answer Gail was expecting, after reflection, this was her takeaway:

> Are we spending all of our time on potato chip decisions and wondering why we don't have any energy left for the good stuff?

And, here is my takeaway:

> **Are we wondering why people don't have any energy left for the good stuff when all we're giving them are potato chip decisions?** (If you didn't just say "aha" aloud to yourself, you need to go back and reread the question.)

Practically speaking:

- The more elements you put on a page, the less important each element becomes.

- The more announcements you have from a platform, the less people hear.

- The more brochures you add to the pile, the harder it is for people to find what they're looking for.

- The more ministry or organizational logos you create, the less meaningful the overall church or organizational identity becomes.

Now I like potato chips as much as the next person, but I argue this is a principle of stewardship; are you responsible with information you have to share?

IS CHOICE REALLY SUCH A GOOD THING?

In theory, more choices may lead people to find exactly what they want. But, research shows people actually feel worse. Too much choice leads to one of three results: regret, shutdown or paralysis. It looks different depending on the generational attributes, but "give them more choices" is often an ineffective communication strategy for anyone.

- Baby boomers get overwhelmed and shutdown.

- GenXers think they want the choices (and expect them) but labor over whether or not they're making the right decision.

- GenYers just ignore you and move on to something that really interests them.*

That said, demographics don't tell the story like behavior. Our brains are rewiring on the fly—adapting to new ways of life. I know that I for one don't fit perfectly into any one of these categories. And, my response to too many choices depends on the circumstance. I've experienced them all.

And, if I know what it feels like, I'm wondering if you do, too?

At least once a year, we have a weekend message series about volunteering. It's when we throw the net out far and wide, educating and encouraging the people in our church to find their fit on a ministry team. We've tested various vehicles to help equip people with the information they need to make a move. I fondly

---

* "Baby boomer" is the term used to describe people born during the baby boom between 1946 and 1964. They were the first group raised with televisions in the home. The GenX generation was following the baby boom. Generation X thinking has significant overtones of cynicism against things held dear to the previous generations, mainly the baby boomers. GenY individuals were born roughly between 1982 and 1994. The rise of instant communication technologies and media has potentially shaped their reputation for being peer-oriented and for seeking instant gratification.

remember one of those vehicles several years ago—a bulletin insert for our Ministry Fair.

I helped pull together the content for this insert. By the time we were done, it was four pages, single-spaced, with every team and volunteer role that existed in our church. And, I was proud. Logically, this made sense, right? People don't serve because they don't know what's available. If we show them *everything* that's available—the hundreds of opportunities to choose from—they'll be able to find what they're looking for.

Sound familiar?

What we learned is that people aren't motivated to move in the face of hundreds of choices. In fact, they were being frazzled about where to start and left feeling overwhelmed. The next year, we condensed the copy from more than fifty teams into eight categories.

Before: two of four total pages.

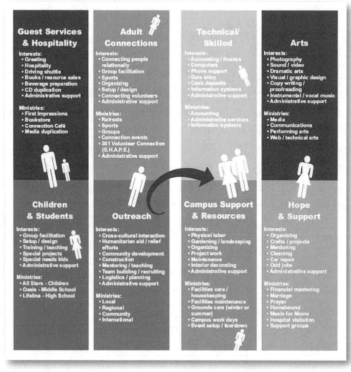

Guest Services & Hospitality
Interests:
• Greeting
• Hospitality
• Driving shuttle
• Books / resource sales
• Beverage preparation
• CD duplication
• Administrative support

Ministries:
• First Impressions
• Bookstore
• Connection Café
• Media duplication

Adult Connections
Interests:
• Connecting people relationally
• Group facilitation
• Sports
• Organizing
• Setup / design
• Connecting volunteers
• Administrative support

Ministries:
• Retreats
• Sports
• Groups
• Connection events
• 301 Volunteer Connection (S.H.A.P.E.)
• Administrative support

Technical/ Skilled
Interests:
• Accounting / finance
• Computers
• Phone support
• Data entry
• Cash deposits
• Information systems
• Administrative support

Ministries:
• Accounting
• Administrative services
• Information systems

Arts
Interests:
• Photography
• Sound / video
• Dramatic arts
• Visual / graphic design
• Copy writing / proofreading
• Instrumental / vocal music
• Administrative support

Ministries:
• Media
• Communications
• Performing arts
• Web / technical arts

Children & Students
Interests:
• Group facilitation
• Setup / design
• Training / teaching
• Special projects
• Special needs kids
• Administrative support

Ministries:
• All Stars - Children
• Oasis - Middle School
• Lifeline - High School

Outreach
Interests:
• Cross-cultural interaction
• Humanitarian aid / relief efforts
• Community development
• Construction
• Mentoring / teaching
• Team building / recruiting
• Logistics / planning
• Administrative support

Ministries:
• Local
• Regional
• Community
• International

Campus Support & Resources
Interests:
• Physical labor
• Gardening / landscaping
• Organizing
• Project work
• Maintenance
• Interior decorating
• Administrative support

Ministries:
• Facilities care / housekeeping
• Facilities maintenance
• Grounds care (winter or summer)
• Campus work days
• Event setup / teardown

Hope & Support
Interests:
• Organizing
• Crafts / projects
• Mentoring
• Cleaning
• Car repair
• Odd jobs
• Administrative support

Ministries:
• Financial mentoring
• Marriage
• Prayer
• Homebound
• Meals for Moms
• Hospital visitation
• Support groups

After: one page.

And, a few people got nervous. "Why don't we provide a way for people to select from all of the individual roles available? How will people find us?"

Here is how we explained the minimalistic approach.

> People are busy and life is hard. They have too much information bombarding them from everywhere (not just one hour on Sunday) and never enough time. But, they're still looking for answers that make a real difference in their lives. Being part of something bigger than you makes a difference. And, people experience that life change one step at a time. *The value we provide grows in direct proportion to how easily people can find and say yes to their next step.*

And, the opposite is true: the value we provide decreases in direct proportion to how hard we make it for people to do what they're trying to do.

The minimalistic approach here is all about breaking a big leap into smaller, incremental steps. A person's journey away from God does not happen in one step, but rather in a series of steps and decisions that seemed otherwise perfectly rational at the time. One day, he wakes up and realizes just how far he's traveled as a result of the sum total of steps in the wrong direction. And, what about when he's ready to start taking steps back? How hard are we making it for him?

YOUR NEW IS NOT NEWS

I commonly get questions about how to "launch" new Web sites, newsletters or logos. My answer is always the same—don't talk about it; just do it. If it's good, people will notice. More to the point, a Web site, newsletter (online or off), or logo is not newsworthy in itself. It just helps deliver the newsworthy items. Talking about it is just goofy.

Katya Andresen, veteran marketer and nonprofit professional, puts it this way.

> "You should not communicate what is new in your universe. You should communicate what matters to your constituents. If you have a new logo or brand* look-and-feel, that's nice, but it doesn't mean a thing to the outside world. What matters to the outside world is how they experience you.

> If you have a new newsletter or Web site, figure out what is incredibly interesting IN that newsletter or Web site. Show what your audience members can do that they could not before."[6]

You know how it would be poor form to hog the spotlight when you give someone a gift? You would never say, "Look at me and the gift I picked out! Isn't that just the greatest news ever?" (At least I hope you wouldn't.) It's kind of like that when you update your logo, newsletter or Web site. **Just give someone the gift without trying to bring attention to yourself.**

---

* In this context, "brand" is referring to the collection of descriptive verbal attributes and symbols (e.g., name, logo, slogan, design) you use to convey the essence of your church, product or service.

LESS PROMOTIONS = MORE PUBLICITY

Instead of asking what you can create to get the word out, what if you asked the opposite? After all, it's about the quality of an experience, not the quantity of promotional items. Consider these stats.

Which makes you most comfortable purchasing a product?
  8% Web site
 15% Advertisement
 22% Newspaper
 76% A friend recommended it[7]

Best source for advice on a new product[8]
 21% Television
 26% Newspaper/Magazine
 35% Info Services (Consumer Reports)
 67% Another consumer who owns the product

I trust this type of advertising[9]
 45% Radio
 45% Television
 50% Magazine
 90% Recommendations from consumers

What does each of these illustrations have in common? **The best promotion is a satisfied customer.**

In *Branding Faith*,[10] Phil Cooke says, "Yesterday it was about dumping the same message on the mass audience because they didn't have much choice. Today, it's about making a connection—the kind of connection that not only makes people want to hear what you have to say, but also makes them respond."

So, instead of dumping the same message on the masses, what if we get back in touch with what people are connecting with and develop our approach from there?

We don't put a lot of weight on advertising, flyers and brochures to get the word out at our church. Occasionally, we will invest efforts for special promotions, but primarily, we focus our time, energy and money on two things to get the word out.

1. **Satisfied customers.** Give people an experience to talk about. They'll tell their friends so you don't have to. (For us, it's the weekend service.)

2. **Invite tools.** Give satisfied customers a variety of tools to help make it easier for them to tell their friends. (For us, it's the series postcard and service clips on our Web site.)

THINK IT OVER

Busting the myth—the more choices the better.

☐ How can I offer my audience the ability to use their natural decision triggers? What can I do to make it easy for people to say yes to the next small step?

☐ Am I responsibly managing the information I have by giving people only the best, or am I contributing to information overload by burdening people with potato chip decisions?

☐ Where am I bombarding people with information and draining their ability to be inspired?

☐ Which communication vehicles in my church or organization are most effective and why? Which tools would not be missed if they were gone? Can I identify communication pieces that exist purely to serve the internal politics of the organization?

☐ If I evaluate the last three communication pieces I created, how much was simple and succinct? How much was detail overkill?

chapter 3

THE MYTH: ADVERTISING CREATES INTEREST

Advertising doesn't create interest; at best, it creates awareness. And, that is not always a good thing. Cancer has awareness, and nobody wants that. Yankelovich, a consumer market research firm, revealed this in the results of its marketing receptivity survey:

Nearly 70% of consumers say they are interested in products that enable them to block out advertising.

I heard about another national research survey asking the American public what top five things need more government regulation. Get this: advertising was ranked #4—after air pollution and before *nuclear safety*! What people want is a promise they can trust, consistency, something worth telling their friends about—an experience. Instead of investing efforts in promotions to get attention, we should be getting attention with what happens when people show up.

TRANSPARENCY

One way to help keep a team aligned is to broaden perspective as a team; get in touch with "customers" and culture. And, to be successful in the process, it's important to foster an environment that allows honesty about what people discover—inside and outside of themselves.

Are you and the people on your team willing to share what they see or hear *transparently* with each other? Do you foster a safe environment for candid, constructive observations even if they are unpleasant or uncomfortable?

Here's an excerpt from an email I received from a key leader in our church. He sent it in response to the question "what do you think contributes to the decline in local Church attendance?" He is strong in his faith; committed to the mission, vision and values of our church; dependable; and high capacity. And, he is *transparent* about his risky observations about the Church.

> ### ✉ NEW EMAIL
>
> Sometimes I feel the Church over-promises and under-delivers. I guess that's part of feeling as if you've been sold a bill of goods. It promises love, joy, peace and purpose. It says give and you'll receive. It says be a good person and good things will happen to you. Become a Christian and your life will change. Yeah, sorta…
>
> It reminds me of a network marketing organization (many of which, by the way, are launched within church setting). You have a bunch of people who aren't good at sales out trying to sell with a little bit of information about their product. They over-hype and make promises they can't possibly keep. It's a second-class, circus-like sales organization that people don't take seriously. "Oh. It's a network marketing company? Great. You're one of those people." "Oh. You're telling me I need church and God? Great. You're one of those people."
>
> After all, liberals have a valid argument about the "Christian Right," don't they? Divorce rates are similar. My own daughter is in spiritual limbo after growing up in the church. My in-laws are on the brink of divorce. My wife

and I still have fights and have hard times "on the brink." I'm estranged from my best friend and haven't spoken with him in years. I've had business failures. I've felt crushed under the burden of debt. Hmmm. Yeah. I'm much better off than people who don't go to church and those who don't tithe!

Why do so many Christians sell Jesus "pain-relievers"? Man, I must have missed that pill. He does rescue. He does save. But, I still feel pain. And, so did He.

So what is it? What is it that truly adds that value to life? For one, I have to remind myself "it's not about here." Our life on earth is temporary and our purpose is not an unwavering pursuit of happiness, wealth and health here…NO! We struggle, we work it out and we deal with it. We're not immune to it…but our hope, prize and purpose is and will be with Christ. Shame on us for over-selling life here on earth.

Can the church offer happiness? Healing? Financial relief? Longer life? Christian kids? Can it promise the fruits of the Spirit without being the Spirit? Many do.

What is it that we can truly promise a seeker or a believer? I could go on, but I'll stop there for now. I believe we can do better. We just need a better plan.

Being transparent is not only being honest about who you are, it is also about being honest about how you are perceived by others. **It's risky, but worth it. It could make the difference between high-impact and no impact at all.**

BE ATTRACTIVE.

Only when you're *attractive* will you have the ability to *attract*. To *attract* is to cause to approach or adhere. If you have a message you're sending out, isn't it worth the extra effort to make the message attractive? Let's use Moe's Southwest Grill as a case study for *attraction*.

In the summer of 2008, the American public had a tomato scare. The media reported about the number of people becoming sick from eating tomatoes contaminated with salmonella bacteria was rising. Our local Moe's, like many other restaurants and businesses in the food industry, had to get a message out about their tomatoes. They displayed the same messages two ways. I snapped these photos on my mobile phone camera to show both.

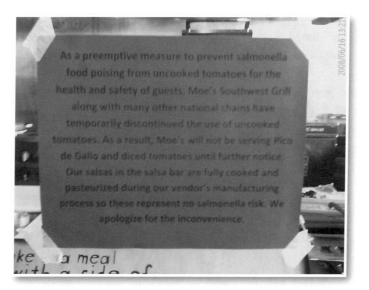

Ugly. I didn't even notice it was there. Walked right by it, even though it was on bright red paper. When I did read it, I was bored.

Attractive! No bright color or expensive surgery. Just having some fun with a simple message. I noticed it right away. I appreciate the fact that somebody took the extra time to "look good for company."

I have no idea why they needed both signs (side by side, even) when they say the exact same thing. But, it is a great comparison for us—*a tale of two tomatoes.* **Which one will you be?**

WHO DO YOU LOVE MORE—
THE WHAT OR THE WHO?

We should be asking ourselves this question in all communication efforts. Am I more attached to *what* I have to say than *how* I say it? Everywhere in our life—whether it's at work or play, internal or external—people tune out if the content is abrupt, lofty, bossy or boring. If they're in a bad place, they might even rebel against the pettiest things.

Even if it's just a sign you hang in your corporate kitchen. People are more inclined to read and respond if there's something in it for them—a laugh, a reward, a compassionate tone delivered from their point-of-view.

Recently, we needed to roll out a new employee handbook at our staff meeting. You know the drill—hundreds of pages full of boring policies and procedures. But, there was also important new information everyone needed to observe whether they knew it or not, whether they cared or not.

The easiest thing to do would have been to simply hand out the manual and tell everyone they had to read it. Instead, our executive pastor, Tim Stevens, took the extra time to consider his audience. He dedicated time to prepare a careful presentation that valued the message recipients.

This is just part of the pop quiz he created to roll out the new staff handbook to the team. We had a blast at that staff meeting. Everybody laughed and interacted; it was amazing to observe people having a merry ol' time around the *employee handbook*.

If you don't know how to add inspiration and motivation to your information, find somebody around you to help. Everybody needs an image consultant. Even for kitchen signs and employee handbooks. (And tomatoes!)

Employee Handbook – POP QUIZ

Students, be sure to use a #2 pencil or Sharpie Magnum. Carefully listen to each question and then circle the letter of the correct answer, which, by the way, is "C." Yes, that's right, the correct answer for every question is letter "C". Cheating is encouraged.

Do not work ahead of the class. Your teacher (the bald, good-looking guy at the front of the class) will lead the class in reading each question.

1. I need to sign an acknowledgement stating I've read the new handbook because...

   a. I'm not trusted.

   b. Some lawyer says its' a good idea.

   c. There's some new stuff I need to know.

2. There is a section called the "Statement of Ethics" in the handbook that outlines...

   a. How to ethically cheat on your taxes.

   b. When I need to wear my seatbelt.

   c. The rules of the game for staff members of GCC—they will keep you from being sidelined due to perception of wrong doing. (Pages 11-12)

3. When it says that we maintain an "at will" employment policy, it means...

   a. You must do anything your supervisor asks (i.e. like wash their car or polish their shoes).

   b. You work for free.

   c. It is legalese that complies with Indiana hiring law and means you don't need a reason to quit and GCC doesn't need a reason to terminate your employment. (Page 13)

A page from the Granger Community Church Employee Handbook Pop Quiz.

ADMIT IT. YOU LIKE PEOPLE
WHO ARE LIKE YOU.

Stephen Denny is a marketing expert with 20 years proven performance, connecting brands to the wants and needs of technology users. He's helped manage the people, strategy and budgets at brand name companies such as Sony, OnStar and Iomega. I consistently read his blog, note-to-cmo.blogspot.com, to gain insight from conversations he has with very smart colleagues, clients and readers. In one of his posts, he took a picture with his mobile phone camera to capture an example of how one business was finding things in common with their audience.

Snapped outside Starbucks.[1]

"Did you know that Starbucks is just like you? They use 2% milk, too. You guys apparently have something in common! And that's great.

Consider the alternatives. They could have said, *We only serve 2% milk. Whole or skim on request (or extra).* They could have just switched and not told anyone."

It's not rocket science—got milk? **Businesses work hard to think like their customers to find simple ways to connect. Don't you think we should work harder at this virtue, too?**

IT'S NOT WHAT YOU SAY;
IT'S WHAT PEOPLE HEAR.

If you advertise a "product" without taking into consideration all the things that happen when someone comes in contact with that product (or any part of your organization), it can actually work against you. What we say to address one group of people can actually alienate another. Sometimes, it's worth it. The objective is not to try to please the world. However, it is helpful to evaluate if it needs to be said in a different setting or if it needs to be said at all.

I got to thinking about this when Rusty Weston, a writer for *Fast Company* magazine, devoted an entire article[2] to his perception of "Christian staffing." Here are just a few excerpts from that article.

Christian staffing. Do you work in a predominantly Christian workplace? Increasingly, Christian job boards are making this mission, as some put it, a reality.

My take on the job boards that match "followers" with "Christian employers" is that a Christian workplace is at least partially about excluding non-believers who may undermine their value system.

This statement on *Christian Staffing's* Web site summarizes the mindset: "Have you dealt with staff problems including stealing, fraud, sexual harassment, lack of work ethic, tardiness, etc? We did, and so we have decided to try to hire people we knew had a good reputation...and more specifically followers of Jesus Christ."

What is unclear to me is how a Christian employee

differs from, say, a Hindu, Islamic or Jewish employee. Of course, it's no secret that religious cultures and subcultures often hire amongst themselves; what's different here is these job boards are explicit about it.

Biases are part of the American fabric, right? The federal government, including the U.S. Justice Department, recruits from Christian law schools and colleges. (That hasn't gone so well.)

For many cultures and subcultures, a homogeneous, immersive environment is the most appealing way to live and work. But where are the winners here? People who seek faith-based work environments lose the value of collaborating with people from different cultures, who offer different ideas and perspectives; and people who are excluded from faith-based workplaces may be victims of discrimination.

The justification for a Christian staffing source is not what caught this writer's attention. It's how it's talked about.

Sometimes, we can't see it ourselves—that message we unintentionally send. It helps to hear an outsider's perspective. Playwright Anton Chekhov said, "Man will become better when you show him what he's like." I know it's true. **Who you are is important but don't underestimate the value of how you are perceived.**

DON'T BRAND—BOND

Of the general population, 7% believes that companies tell the truth in advertising.[3] So, how do you get through to the other 93% in this low-trust, high-volume world? Simple. You cut out all the extras, so the real message can be heard.

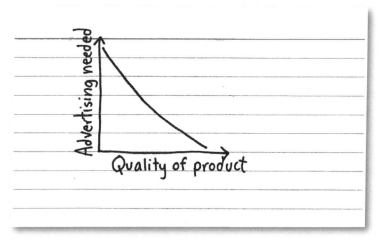

From Jessica Hagy's blog.[4]

People don't want to hear about what the corporate copy says is going to happen. They want to hear it from their friends or just experience it for themselves. Your job? Eliminate the weight of bullhorn self-promotion, and make your offering easy to find. And, if what they find is worthwhile, it will speak for itself.

Stick to the facts, and dispense with the fluff. **Clarity is the new creativity.**

THINK IT OVER

Busting the myth—advertising creates interest.

☐ Do I foster an environment that allows honesty about what people discover—inside and outside of themselves? Am I, or the people around me, willing to be transparent and share what we see even when it's uncomfortable and hard to understand?

☐ Am I more attached to what I have to say than how I say it? Do I have someone around me that can help identify if my content is abrupt, lofty, bossy, boring or out-of-touch before I finalize it?

☐ Am I actively learning what new trends are and how these trends are changing the way people are doing life? Who can help me in my discovery?

☐ Is there a simpler or more compelling way to communicate our message?

☐ What am I overselling? Where do we, as a church or an organization, under-deliver?

chapter 4

THE MYTH: IT WORKED BEFORE SO IT WILL WORK AGAIN

Every organization has to face a changing culture, and your audience is changing faster than you are. In the past, mass marketing reached a captive audience. It was easy to do with only three network TV channels, no Internet, email, satellite radio, cable TV or TiVo.* Now, mass marketing doesn't reach the masses because the masses are spread out and tuning out. People are ignoring sterilized marketing copy and looking for recommendations from their friends. They're supplementing face-to-face interpersonal relationships with online social networks. You can ignore the current reality and use old techniques you're comfortable with, imitate new techniques that discredit you as a fraud or take the time to learn what's effectively gaining credibility with people in today's culture.

---

* TiVo® has completely changed the television experience. It's a hard drive you connect to your TV almost like a VCR, except it's always on. All the TV you watch is through the TiVo, and it allows you to record anything you want, whenever you want. It allows you to pause and rewind live TV, skip commercials, find and record things by actor or keyword, etc.

ARE YOU TOO FAMILIAR?

You wouldn't expect to find parallels between the video game development and ministry discipline, but that's exactly what I found when I read a *WIRED* magazine article about Halo 3.*

I was inspired by three particular strategies of the game's development team.

1. They watched people play the game and made notes of problem areas they, as the game creators, were too close to see. They watched facial expressions, body language and player results, tracking everything from favored weapons to how and where players most frequently get killed.

As a result, they discovered flaws between what the game creators *thought people should do* and *what they actually did*. They went back and corrected bugs and graphics that were ineffective.

2. They analyzed the change in their team dynamic and processes in the face of growth. When they started developing Halo, they could all sit in a single room and communicate by yelling over their shoulders or peer at each other's cool creations on screen.

As a result, they discovered the pressure to deliver Halo 2 nearly destroyed them. Separate teams formed to design each level of the game, but they didn't coordinate their efforts. When they assembled all of their pieces for the first time, they discovered that the story was incomprehensible. They actually had the guts to throw out 80% of their work and start over.

* Halo 3, a first-person shooter video game, grossed $300 million in its first week. More than one million people played Halo 3 on Xbox Live in the first 20 hours. As of January 3, 2008, Halo 3 has sold 8.1 million copies, and it was the best-selling video game of 2007 in the U.S.

3. They watched the stats and looked for positive and negative trends. These trends were one of the probes they used to find trouble.

As a result, one report revealed an unusual number of "suicides" among the players piloting the alien Wraith tank in an upper level. They discovered that the firing line of the guns was misaligned and inadvertently killing (and frustrating) the players. They went back and fixed the guns and the suicides stopped.

What do church and organization leaders have to learn from game developers?

- Every stakeholder aims for the same goal: keep players in a "flow" state—constantly surfing the edges of their abilities without bogging them down. Are we intentional about watching the flow experience for our guests? I'm reminded to create space to watch people experience our creations—watch facial expressions, body language and traffic patterns the first time they encounter a touchpoint at our church. Last weekend, I sat on the far right of our auditorium and watched people as they read (or didn't read) the bulletin. I observed them at different points in the service for positive (or negative) responses. I watched where people went and listened to what they said as they left the auditorium after service. I was a spy.

- Game makers devise a system with a few basic rules, goals and equipment for the journey—constructing environments that influence the behavior of the people inside them. In other words, they give people the tools, clear the way and allow people to find their own way of achieving their goals. Do we provide the tools and create the environments for people to find their own way to connect with resources and each other? Or, do we prescribe rules, force paths and do their thinking for them?

- Game makers eliminated battlefield areas where players were bored, stuck, or killed—they were simply baffled about where to go. They took notice when players were doing things the designers never thought of. They altered worlds in small ways to subtly direct player movement. Do we dismiss people who don't take the path we think they should, or are we looking for innovative ways to change our world, solve open-ended problems and save lives?

- Game makers watch the stats to find what's working and what's broken. Do we plow ahead making assumptions and support needs that don't exist? Recently, our reports revealed that four out of 5,000 people from the weekend service accessed our online discussion guides. That information allowed us to redirect the writing team to places where they could make a bigger impact.

Who said computer games are a waste of time? The developers of Halo 3 have just modeled the way to change lives. We can learn something from them.

CREATE CONVERSATIONS, NOT CONTENT

It's the conversation economy, stupid. Oh, I'm not calling you stupid. That's the title of an article[1] I read in *Business Week* magazine about *conversation architecture*. Consider these thoughts from the article:

Once upon a time, we were consumers. We took in the messages that were communicated to us. We didn't really get to talk back.

Marketing has traditionally been about messages. Now consider this: the medium is the message.[2]

Great experiences are a start, but they aren't enough. Communities are forming around popular social platforms such as YouTube, Facebook, Flickr, Ning, Twitter—the list goes on and on. These platforms facilitate conversation. Conversation leads to relationships and relationships lead to affinity.

Emerging media is changing how we interact with each other and with brands. Does this sound like marketing? Well, it is. It's how we market to each other. Yes, that's right—we market to each other. We always have, in fact, but now, we're doing it in a more digitally connected way. We swap stories about products and services we like or dislike. We share knowledge and expertise. We define a new kind of currency fueled by conversation and founded in meaningful relationships.

I can imagine what some of you might be thinking as you read this. "Why does any of this apply to me? I'm not a computer person—I'm in ministry. I don't understand all that technology stuff. Conversation architecture? You might as well be speaking Greek to me."

I remember when I was in fourth grade; we had a week of indoor recess. The teachers allowed us to bring games and music from home to share and stay entertained.* I couldn't wait to take my favorite album in to share with everyone. It was my parents' album, *The Very Best of Herman's Hermits,* and I knew every word of every song by heart. I just knew everyone in the class would love it as much as I did. I imagined the smiles and laughter we would all share singing along to "Henry the Eighth" and "I'm into Something Good." So, when the day finally came, I was horrified at the reaction I got from my classmates. It was nothing like I had dreamed it would be. No one appreciated or enjoyed the music I brought to share—*at all.* Instead, they laughed at and ridiculed me for being such an out-of-touch loser. Nobody wanted to hang out with me after the "Herman's Hermits" incident. I was a laughingstock, and it took years to recover. My intentions were good. My heart was pure. But, it didn't matter because I was speaking in a language nobody understood— playing music nobody else was listening to. I tried to get noticed using my parents' music.

So what is the church or your organization to do in this new generation? (Notice I said "in" this new generation, not "with"... because like it or not, we're *in* it.) Here's a paraphrase of what the online experts are saying. [3]

- Think services, not Web sites.

- Connect (not control) people.

- Do not expect people to come to you online any more; go to where people are online.

---

* Now would be a good time to grab a tissue.

If you have ever said, "I just don't get computers" or "I'm not into all that online stuff," then you have announced to the world that you are out-of-touch. Even if you're not ready to start interacting online, you have a responsibility at least to go online to watch others interact.

Life change happens in relationships, and this new human behavior is all about developing relational collateral online. *Conversation architecture* is one of the most important issues facing ministry and other organizations today. If we don't find a way to meet people in their online spaces (e.g., texting, Facebook, blogs), we end up having conversations with ourselves.

You know what psychiatrists will call you for that, don't you? Crazy.

And, fourth graders will call you a loser. (I'm still not over it.)

WHAT HAPPENED TO OUR ATTENTION SPANS?

The BBC claims the addictive nature of web browsing can leave you with an attention span of nine seconds—the same as a goldfish.[4] It makes sense to me. Did you know your brain rewires itself based on how you use it? Our attention span—brain functioning—is affected by the way we do things. Generations of people are developing the habit of not concentrating.

Josh Catone, a developer and blogger at an online media company, had this to say about it in an article[5] he wrote:

Twitter* reduces our thoughts to just 140 characters. 12seconds.tv does it in 12 seconds. The average length of the 12 billion online videos consumed by U.S. users in May? 2.7 minutes.

The more words you add to a page the more people skim it. Our short attention spans can't handle long articles, and we end up just skipping to the bottom.

Shorter blog posts or posts chunked with headlines, bullet points or images get more comments than posts with lengthy blocks of text.

Television, the internet and other external stimuli has rewired our brains to make it harder to absorb information that doesn't come in bite-sized chunks. Our brains are ready to jump to the next stimuli before we've fully absorbed the first.

* Twitter is an online network that allows people to send and read each other's updates (known as tweets). You can follow updates on your computer or mobile phone. In fact, you can follow my tweets at twitter.com/kemmeyer.

I've read and heard the hubbub* about how the Internet is making us stupid. Or, how people need to get a life and turn off the computer. In this same article, Josh says, "We need to stop focusing on getting so much information, so quickly. It's okay to miss some things. It's okay not to put up a post about every breaking story as soon as it happens. It's okay not to tweet everything you see or do. It's okay not to have 5,000 friends."

I wouldn't disagree with that. However, our reality isn't all or nothing.

My take? **The Internet isn't making us dumb; it's making us different.** And, it's not that we just need to unplug to stay smart. It's that we need to flip flop how we supplement our knowledge. That is, in the past we had to create the space to *log on* to enhance our learning and social networks. Now, we need to create the space to *log off* to do the same.

We need to acknowledge that our brains process information differently today than they did five years ago. And, if we intend to be helpful, we should audit our communications perspective to determine if we're presenting too much information to be absorbed.

Recently, my team reviewed our own weekly bulletin, enewsletter and Web site with fresh eyes. In the process, we found paragraphs and pages of content we had added over time that people weren't noticing. And, if they're not noticing them, they're not using them. Bloated content doesn't make a powerful impact, so we made cuts. We killed and combined pages because it was the responsible thing to do.

* Who can say "hubbub" without snickering? Not me.

THAT'S NOT HOW I REMEMBER IT

I came home from work and found this picture on my desk with a note from my son, Easton (seven years old at the time).

Apparently, he was designing new logos for Google, and he wanted me to send his designs in to them for consideration.

It got me thinking about some of the things that are part of normal, daily life for my kids that didn't exist when I was growing up. Besides Google, there are:

- **User names.** My kids were in first and third grade when I first heard them in the backseat talking about various user names for their classmates. This is not what my friends and I talked about on the bus growing up.

- **GPS (Global Positioning System):** My best guess is that God created Dora the Explorer* so kids can learn what maps are actually used for.

- **Channel 31.** My kids have hundreds of television channels to choose from. I had five.

- **Code blue drills.** When I was growing up, we had fire drills. My kids have drills to protect themselves from terrorist attacks.

I'm familiar with most of what the kids are talking about today, but it's less than it was a year ago and I imagine that gap will grow as they do. When I find myself clueless about words they're using, I'm actively researching to learn what they're all about. I can't afford to write it off to "kids these days," or I'll lose touch with their culture. And, to tell you the truth, it's easier than ever to learn *anything* about *everything* with a Google search. I land on these sites the most during my "research."

- Wikipedia.com Searchable Internet encyclopedia.

- UrbanDictionary.com A searchable archive of contemporary American slang,** listed in alphabetical order.

- azLyrics.com Searchable song lyrics database.

When I'm engaged in their culture, I can stay in relationship with them. This is true of your audience as well… whether that is your spouse, your staff, your church, or your neighbor. Think about it.

---

* Dora the Explorer is a successful cartoon for preschoolers on the Nickelodeon cable channel. The Map is a supporting character on every episode, providing travel guidance and advice.

** This site should be rated R for mature audiences. As with any slang, some definitions get racy. There is no obscenity filter included.

MOBILE CULTURE

I pulled into the church parking lot today and saw a car parked sideways with a woman slumped over in her seat. Five years ago, I would have stopped my car immediately to offer assistance, knowing she was either crying, passed out, or dead. Today, I just drove right on by. I didn't even slow down. I knew she was just bent over texting on her mobile phone. Here are some revealing truths about our mobile-device culture.[6]

- Many people rock their earbuds at high volume to avoid human interaction.

- Commuters plug in because they don't want to be where they are.

- iPods create a sphere of physical isolation.

- Americans tend to be a little touchy about their personal space.

Do you think people are addicted to technology? Do you think social media and texting are "replacing" real relationships? Are you afraid people don't know how to have a conversation anymore? Does it annoy you that people can't turn off their cell phones for an hour?

Kelley Hartnett is the Director of Communications at Morning Star Church in Missouri. She recently wrote about her "Rela-tech-ship"[7] and how it has *enhanced* her relationships, not *replaced* them.

I'm connecting with people—more frequently and more consistently than I ever have. In the last few days, I've gotten real-time updates from friends about a death in the family, a sudden hospitalization, a first-ever home-coming date and reactions to the presidential debate. I learned that a quiet church guy has an incredible wit, and I discovered that another church guy and I share the same wacky taste in music. All of my in-person interactions with these folks have an undercurrent of community that I'd not experienced before.

I'm learning from people—more effectively and more efficiently that I ever have. By paying attention to other church communications professionals, I'm discovering what conferences I need to attend and what books I need to read. During a recent media aftermath, I tweeted an SOS to my social media guru friend who was able to offer immediate, sage advice. And because all of those people know other people, I have a virtually unlimited, instantly accessible network of really smart people at my disposal.

I'm loving people—more authentically and more freely than I ever have. Sure, that sounds a little Lucy-in-the-sky-with-diamonds, but it's true. Yes, it would be great if we could have backyard BBQs with our buddies every evening. But given our overloaded schedules, that's not realistic. Yes, it's nice to pick up the phone and call someone to offer a kind word and some encouragement. But no one's ever home. In the last week, I've visited someone in the hospital as a direct result of a tweet asking for prayer. I've sent a congratulations message to a teenager. I "LOLd"* with a friend whom I haven't talked with in a while. I got to "listen" to one of my dearest friends express a new level of vulnerability.

* Laugh out loud (LOL).

All of this new technology can appear threatening at first. But, now you've heard another side of the story. And, the more you learn, the more you will discover that culture hasn't shut down, it has just shifted and the space in which we interact looks different.

THINK IT OVER

Busting the myth—it worked before so it will work again.

- ☐ Are we providing tools, creating the environment, and allowing people to find their own way to connect with next steps and each other? Or, do we prescribe rules, force paths and do their thinking for them?

- ☐ Do I dismiss people who are baffled about where to go, don't do things the way I think they should, or respond in ways I didn't anticipate? Or, do I look for new ways to open the flow and eliminate frustrations?

- ☐ And are we confident enough in our mission to discard "battlefield areas" where people are bored and stuck?

- ☐ Am I resistant to watch the new environments where people are interacting online before I jump to conclusions? Am I so egocentric that I believe my perspective is the only one that matters?

- ☐ What are we doing to learn about new methods and trends to understand how and why people are drawn to them?

- ☐ Can I identify the *Very Best of Herman's Hermit's* in my organization? What out of date tool are we blindly holding on to because of habit?

THE MYTH: PEOPLE CARE ABOUT WHAT YOU SAY

You think people care about what you have to say? The truth is that the average person doesn't notice you. And, if they happen to have a different point of view than you do, they'll flat out dismiss you as a non-option. It's not that you're not likeable or smart; it's just a matter of survival for people in today's world. There is simply too much out there and not enough time to take it all in. Spotty memories and decreased benevolence are on the rise, and people are shutting down in an effort to make it through another day. The last thing they're looking for is unsolicited information or someone to tell them to change their ways. They, however, will take time to read or hear something that reinforces an opinion they already have or speaks to a real need in their life. If they're not looking for it, they won't hear it. But, if you take the time to learn what they're looking for, you can get in on a conversation already in process.

EMOTIONAL IGNORANCE

Dr. Mark Goulston, author of *Get Out of Your Own Way: Overcoming Self-Defeating Behavior*, shares a list of misconceptions about how others view you and ten more about how you view others. It's a perfect illustration of what you don't know can hurt you. Don't you want to know?

Absorb it to significantly influence self-awareness and increase favorable interactions with others. **Ignore it at your own peril.**

Misconceptions of How Others View You:

Believing you are:	When perceived by others as:
Shrewd	Sly
Confident	Arrogant
Humorous	Inappropriate
Energetic	Hyper
Having strong opinions	Opinionated
Passionate	Impulsive
Strong	Rigid
Detail-oriented	Nit-picking
Quiet	Passive or indecisive

Misconceptions You Have About Others:

Assuming they are:	When they are actually:
Moved by passion	Moved by facts
Moved by facts	Moved by passion
Fun-loving	Serious
Serious	Fun-loving
Looking for a reason to buy in	Looking for a reason to buy out
Looking for a reason to buy out	Looking for a reason to buy in
Wanting to be told	Wanting to be asked
Needing to be convinced	Ready to buy
Ready to buy	Needing to be convinced
Excited about your organization	Thinking your organization is a dog

I'm pretty sure I'm perceived as arrogant and inappropriate. Little do people know how confidently humorous I really am.

I HAVE ACRONYMPHOBIA

What is it with the need to turn everything into an acronym? I cut this out of a magazine I was flipping through about, of all things, *customer service.*

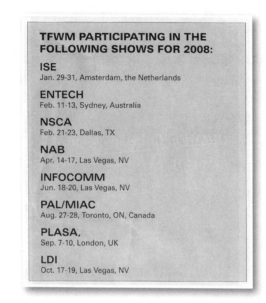

TFWM PARTICIPATING IN THE
FOLLOWING SHOWS FOR 2008:

ISE
Jan. 29-31, Amsterdam, the Netherlands

ENTECH
Feb. 11-13, Sydney, Australia

NSCA
Feb. 21-23, Dallas, TX

NAB
Apr. 14-17, Las Vegas, NV

INFOCOMM
Jun. 18-20, Las Vegas, NV

PAL/MIAC
Aug. 27-28, Toronto, ON, Canada

PLASA,
Sep. 7-10, London, UK

LDI
Oct. 17-19, Las Vegas, NV

And, in case you're wondering, there was no key or legend anywhere in the article to *decode* what these acronyms stood for. I was left wondering what the purpose was for the advertisement. If people don't have the superpower to break the code, this adds no value.

Acronyms happen in the technology and political sectors at an annoying rate. But, it's even more disturbing to see churches frequently use acronyms as an everyday communication practice. Too often, they throw out inscrutable acronyms few people outside their bubble can understand or relate to.

- Do a health check. How many acronyms are in your bulletins, brochures or Web sites?

- Who are you talking to? Are you using a language that only you understand?

- Are you making it easy for guests to find and take their next step?

You can combat this epidemic and change the world. Minimize the use of acronyms in your communications. It has power.

NOBODY'S LISTENING

Making announcements? Whether it's at your service, meeting, or event, there are eight great things you should know about people if you want them to hear what you're saying. This list may not make your job easier, but I guarantee it can help make you more effective.

1. **People aren't open to your change prescription.** Of course, we want to inspire people to be part of something bigger than themselves, to break unhealthy patterns, and live a life of purpose. But, when we dictate "you need to step it up" or "it's time to go deeper," it communicates we have all the answers, and we think people aren't ok where they're starting. They already know they're not as good as they want to be, and we just make it worse. Instead, open their minds and get them thinking. Try "this might be your next step," "here is an opportunity for you to consider," or ask the question "what is your next step?" Remember, everyone's next step looks very different. One person's next step might be to invest or volunteer more but, for another, it may be to finish out the evening without leaving early. And, each of these next steps is equally important.

2. **People aren't motivated by your need.** When people hear "We really need small group leaders" or "We really need your help," they perceive desperation and self-centeredness. And, since they've got needs of their own, your ask feels like one more to add to the pile. Your message should be about the great things that change life for the guest, not about what you (or your church or organization) needs. When you communicate, "Here's a cool opportunity not everyone

knows about" or "You might want to be part of this one-of-a-kind experience," it makes it about them, not us, and it motivates people to move.[*]

3. **People don't know who you are.** It doesn't matter how long you've been around, introduce yourself, every time. Even if it's just for the one new person in the room. When you just get up and start talking, it communicates two things to the guest: exclusivity (everyone's already in the club except for you), and you're pretentious (assuming everyone already knows who you are). Even if it is just a couple of sentences, always take the time to introduce who you are and why you're there.

4. **People multi-task and can't remember squat.** It's human nature to tune out the talking head in the front of the room as you look through your purse, replay the ride there in your mind, or mentally run through your to-do list for what's next. And, if you're lucky enough to have a room full of people with full attention spans who are actually hearing you, there is no guarantee they will remember what you said when they walk out of the room and back into their lives. Visually support your verbal announcement to grab and hold attention, clarify information and raise the interest level of your audience. It doesn't have to be fancy or elaborate. A printed program, PowerPoint slide, table tent, or sign all work fine. Just remember, don't read directly from your visual aids. They're not your script, but a separate component that reinforces your words.

* Speaking of asking for help, have you read *Simply Strategic Volunteers* by Tim Stevens and Tony Morgan? It's a fun, practical and honest book about how to empower people in volunteer ministry.

5. **People are turned off by lack of preparation.** Prepare your announcement so your audience "catches it" within 30 seconds. If it's important enough to announce, then it's important enough to prepare for. Try to cast vision by answering these questions: What is so special about this opportunity? Why should I spend my time on it? How is it going to make my life and me better? Remember, you've got no more than 30 seconds.

6. **People relate when you talk about them or people like them.** Tailor your announcement to your audience. Whenever possible, customize a broad message to a specific audience to make a bigger impact. Even if the announcement doesn't change, it makes all the difference when you find a way to highlight a unique attribute for your specific audience. For example, if you're talking about volunteer opportunities at the food pantry to a group of moms, tell them to bring the kids. If you're talking about the same volunteer opportunity to a group of students, tell them about the donuts that will be there. Help them see how they can specifically use the information you're sharing.

7. **People feel left out and frustrated when you use insider language.** Don't assume everyone is in the know; most people aren't. Avoid the use of acronyms or nicknames. Does everyone know what "The Verge," "TRL," or "Lifeline" is? Be specific and clear, not clever. If it's for middle-schoolers, say so. Once people are on the inside, feel free to use insider language. But, it's never cool to use it in announcements for large groups, connection events, first-serve opportunities, etc. When you do, you can bet that you are alienating guests.

8. **People are not impressed with your technical vocabulary or holy dialect.** Use normal, everyday language. Skip the phrases that are weird and scary to normal people. Don't know what I'm talking about? Picture yourself walking into a professional office setting and trying to have a normal conversation using words such as saved, sanctified and washed in the blood of the lamb. When we use religious words, guests either don't get it or will run from us, so they don't "catch it." Keep it simple and keep it real. Avoid over-spiritualizing and over-complicating your conversation. Your announcements aren't more credible with an entire list of "blessed" or technical phrases.

BIAS AWARENESS

My neighbor "Jim" is one of the nicest people I've ever met. He's outgoing, funny, kind, hard working, family-focused, generous and just an all-around great guy. He makes a difference in his neighborhood and community. Anyone who knows him loves him.

My husband Mark and I stopped by his house one weekend to return some things we had borrowed and caught him in a candid, honest, unguarded moment with friends.

As we listened to him, it became clear that Christians are the reason he doesn't go to church. He was sharing the real-life stories about his interactions with church people—my church—and at one point, he summed it up this way: "I can't stand them."

Jim had always been friendly to us, but guarded. After hearing him say, "I can't stand Christians," it became clear why he had kept a safe distance from us after we moved in. All he knew about us is that I'm on staff at Granger Community Church and that Mark is "heavily involved." I'm sure he had been sitting across the street waiting for us to "pounce" on him like church people. This guy wasn't looking for someone to change his mind.

I get it, my friend. I feel the same way.

Mark and I ate some snacks and stayed awhile with Jim and his friends. We talked about NASCAR, biking, kids, and lack of sleep. We weren't there to sell anything; we just hung out.

And, to be perfectly honest, I respected Jim more for being honest than I would have for being safe and politically correct. I sincerely considered his opinion constructive for all of us.

No one is immune to an outsider's perspective. It doesn't matter if your ministry is progressive and contemporary, traditional and conservative, or relevant and real—**we all have insiders that get in the way of outsiders experiencing Jesus.**

What are you doing to help educate your church body about how others see them?

I CAN'T SEE YOU. OH, WAIT! NOW I CAN.

Chris Forbes is a marketing coach and consultant for faith-based nonprofits, ministries and churches. He has one simple secret for reaching more people: *reach fewer people more times*. Brilliant. Go back. Read it again. Wow.

The secret is for churches and other organizations to narrow their focus and reach fewer people more times. There is more to the secret, of course, than just narrowing your focus on a smaller group of people. You have to understand the people you want to reach. But, because your focus is smaller, this is possible.

This one simple secret is so simple it even works with kittens.

People only pay attention to what their brain tells them they need. For example, when my children were younger, they decided they wanted a pet kitten. We all agreed it would be okay for the children to have a kitten. The next day, I noticed for the first time all the kitten communication in my community. I saw "Kittens for Adoption," "Free Kittens" signs everywhere it seemed. Also, I overheard people even talking about kittens. I even saw stray cats! What made the difference from the day before? On that day, I "needed" a kitten for my daughters.

The fact is people's needs drive what people pay attention to. People usually only notice what will benefit them in some way. As a marketer, you need to understand people's specific needs. When you know who you are trying to reach and begin to understand their needs, your communication can be presented in a way that speaks directly to their needs. That means they will pay attention to your communication and not block it out.[1]

That's the definition of a felt-need—anything people consciously lack, desire or need help with (time and money management, relationships, stress, pain, etc.). Connect with a felt-need, and you will connect with an audience. On the other hand, if you share information without wrapping it around a felt-need, it is almost impossible to make a connection. **Remember, it's easy for people to miss what they're not looking for.**

THINK IT OVER

Busting the myth—people care about what you have to say.

- ☐ Runners strip themselves of any unnecessary weights so they can run unencumbered.[2] What weight is holding me back? Is it a weight of culture? Tradition? Extended family expectations? Or, are there unresolved issues in my heart I need to deal with such as anger, fear, insecurity or jealousy?

- ☐ How many ways can I connect with my audience—naturally, uniquely, and on a one-to-one level? What do I have in common with a parent, a student, a retired person, a neighbor or someone who avoids "church people"? How can I learn to "love the one I'm with"?

- ☐ How would I change a recent presentation I've given or conversation I've had—same room, same slides—if my audience was totally comprised of recent immigrants? From Russia? Who were blind? But loved country music? And were afraid of horses? But loved square dancing? In each case, how would my presentation subtly change?

- ☐ Is our church or organizational communication aligned with our DNA? Are we using the same filter as an overview for everything we create? Is this what we really mean to say? Does it sound like us?

- ☐ What can I do to help educate my church or organization about how others see them? Who can educate me?

part 2

BEST PRACTICES MAKE A DIFFERENCE

I heard it said somewhere that information is giving out but communication is getting through. You should have just had an "aha" moment reading that. If you didn't—go back, and read it again. This is why, as anyone who is trying to communicate, we need to consider our approach. We can't be lazy and speak from our selfish, one-sided point of view if we intend to positively influence perceptions and persuade decisions. A few "best practices"* can help change our vantage point from "what I think needs to be said" to "what my audience thinks they need." Yes, this might be counterintuitive considering most of us typically think we have all the answers, and people don't always know what they need. But, as you'll see, it really works.

* What's a best practice? A reliable technique with proven results.

chapter 6

KNOW YOUR AUDIENCE

If people are struggling to figure out what will make a difference in their daily grind, why would they spend their time and attention on you? In his book, *Get Out of Your Own Way*, Robert Cooper says, "The more you engage with things that inspire you emotionally, the more powerful is your motivation to achieve them." The same is true for your audience. So who are you talking to? Do you even know these people? And, for the record, the answer doesn't lie in demographic insights alone. To communicate effectively with someone, you have to get at the *psychographics*—the attitudes, interests, lifestyles—to connect with the emotion in his or her real world. Only then, will you be able to begin to learn what might make *you* worth his or her time.

CULTURE DEFINED

Years ago when I was working for a regional consulting firm, I attended an internal training class about cross-cultural communication.[2] Although the consultant focused on software development and documentation, my takeaways applied in a variety of contexts. Here's what I uncovered when I recently pulled out my old notes for a fresh opportunity to look at what we do in ministry and why.

> The term culture has been defined in a variety of ways. Even among anthropologists, there is no agreement on a single definition of the term. In fact, researchers Kroeber and Kluckhohn identified over *167 definitions of culture.*"[3]

Wow. That's not 167 cultures, but 167 *definitions of the word.* Interesting.

You know me by now. I'm all about less clutter, less noise. So I'll share six of the 167 definitions. That's more than enough to get us going. Culture is:

- how people think, feel and act.

- a system for creating, sending, storing and processing information developed by human beings.

- a program for behavior.

- the collective programming of the mind, which consists of patterns of thinking, feeling and acting.

- software of the mind.

- the way in which a group of people solves problems.

Too often, I think we're all guilty of defining culture as "the way we do things around here." The good news is we don't have to stay that way.

Historically, the word *culture* derives from the Latin word *colere*, which could be translated "to build," "to care for," "to plant," or "to cultivate."

This is where it gets good. And, this is our opportunity within the church—to use this definition to drive ministry decisions. **Not *this is how we do things around here*, but instead, to build, to care for, to plant or to cultivate.**

THE PSYCHOGRAPHICS INSIDE THE DEMOGRAPHICS

Sociologists, national advertising agencies, consumer-marketing companies and political strategists all use ethnography, the study of living cultures, to explore the social relations that structure everyday lives of society. By observing behaviors "in the field," they learn what it is people want and think they need. They work hard to figure out how they can answer the questions people are asking. They are discovering the space in which people rally, and they go there. They continually learn how to get outside their own bubble to attract and move people to buy products and get votes.

Richard Reising[4] tells a simple story that brilliantly demonstrates what this looks like in a practical way.

A woman is driving down a pitch-dark road late at night and sees that she is almost out of gas. Her fear is somewhat relieved as she sees two gas stations up ahead.

If these two gas stations are equally accessible, and the gas is equally priced, which will she choose?

Simple. She will choose the one with better lighting. Why? At that moment, her primary need is safety.

Better lighting makes her feel safer. Her response is natural—just as natural as the first conclusions that people commonly draw about churches.

Imagine the owner of the less-frequented store. He tries to solve the problem by dropping prices, hiring a new graphic designer, making a new sign and increasing inventory...but his sales do not increase. He is missing the connection. He doesn't understand what drives people.

I have a question for you. How strong is your connection? Is your church providing the right light or are people headed to the other station?* If you don't take the time to learn about your audience, you'll never know.

This may or may not be surprising to you, but many of the primary ethnology research techniques sociologists employ are "soft" and "emotive," not scientific and absolute. They include:

- firsthand observation of daily behavior

- casual conversations and in-depth interviews

- discovery of local beliefs and perceptions

What are you waiting for? Find the answers to these questions, and learn about people that you are trying to reach.

- Why would people want to spend their time and attention in your church instead of the couch, the mall or the club? Consider what they're looking for and rallying around.

- What unique value can people get from you that makes it worth the hassle of changing their schedules? Consider what they can find or experience at your church that they can't anywhere else.

- How does your programming fit into the grind of their lives? Consider the reality of their career demands, sports schedules, financial strain, relationship and family dynamics, etc.

- What is their comfort zone? Consider where they spend their free time and money. Do you know what

* Let's be clear. The "other station" isn't "another church," but "no church." People go to the "other station" every day because the church doesn't have the light on.

they hate and love? Are you aware of the emotional triggers that could attract or repel?*

If you're in ministry, part of your daily discipline should include amateur sociology. Much as intramural sports provide us the opportunity to play collegiate basketball without a scholarship, ministry provides us the opportunity to become ethnographers without a degree. **Really, it should be part of your job description—become a student of people.** And, you know what? It's just not as hard as we make it out to be. **Most of the time, it's as simple as a change of scenery. How can we change our perspective if we don't change our view?** We can't judge our station without trying to see it from the seat of the people driving by.

* Are you wondering what the result of all this questioning looks like? I thought you would be. And, that's why I put a sample of the finished result of Granger's "mindset profile" in a place I affectionately refer to as "the back of the book."

THE WORLD AS YOU SEE IT

I consistently pray and work on renewing my perspective as a spiritual discipline in my life. Let's just say, I never run out of real life situations that challenge me to look at things from somebody else's point of view. Sometimes, I'm intentionally seeking it out. And, other times, it's a hard life lesson I run into face first (like a brick wall).

> "It is the function of art to renew our perception. What we are familiar with we cease to see." —Anaïs Nin

I saw an advertisement in a magazine and immediately thought of how it applied to churches. What a profound illustration to the point.

"Life changes. We've got the wedding pictures to prove it."

What does an old wedding picture with big hair and bad clothes have to do with ministry? Well, to be honest, sometimes, we're still trying to relate to people in a world that no longer exists. Our frame of reference and perspective is as out-of-date as my prom dress from 1986.

So, how do you see the world—as it *is* or the *way you are*? What are you doing to learn about people today who don't see things the way you do? As a church leader, would you be willing to

- go on vacation with an atheist?

- eat dinner at a smoky, local bar with people who swear like truckers?

- listen to secular music (with the explicit label) and learn what the lyrics mean?

- read a racy non-fiction or non-Christian advice book from the *New York Times* Best Seller list?

- make friends with pornographers or strippers?

None of these would be easy. And, they're all uncomfortably controversial. But, sometimes we get so worried about what other church people will say about it, we forget how scripture tells us to live to bring light into the darkness.

The god who rules this world has blinded the minds of unbelievers. They cannot see the light, which is the good news about our glorious Christ, who shows what God is like. We are not preaching about ourselves. Our message is that Jesus Christ is Lord. He also sent us to be your servants. The Scriptures say, "God commanded light to shine in the dark." Now God is shining in our hearts to let you know that his glory is seen in Jesus Christ. (2 Cor. 4:4–6)

I'm just saying, what are you willing to do to learn about people who don't see things the way you do?

DON'T ASSUME THEY'RE BAD APPLES

We're all prone to "fill in the blanks" and make assumptions based on a snapshot. I've done it to others, and it's been done to me. It's particularly easy to do when someone's actions don't match up to what you're used to in your own life. I'm thankful for the hard lessons I've learned in this area, because I jump to conclusions a lot less. I'm learning that the actions don't tell the whole story, and I get the opportunity to dig deeper to learn about the story behind the person—behind the behavior. I'm better because of it and would miss out on SO MUCH that's great in this world if I spent my days running away from, or fighting against, everything new and unknown.

The real boot camp experience for me came when my daughter hit turbulent times in adolescence. I'm convinced those times would have been a lot less turbulent if I hadn't feared some of the new subcultures resonating with her (i.e., the punk scene). I reacted without taking the time to learn about them first. That season when she was fifteen to eighteen years old was enlightening in so many ways. I grew up as much as she did.

I read an article about Shepard Fairey, founder of OBEY Clothing. In it, he talks about his alternative journey and the assumptions that people made about his methods. The insights were helpful.

My whole mode of operation was very similar to skateboarding and punk rock, which was the idea that if the mainstream wasn't picking up on what you were doing, create an alternative scene to the mainstream. My attitude was never "I want to be an isolated person and do my own thing in direct opposition to the mainstream"; it was more like "I need to be doing what I'm doing, and I need to figure out how to keep doing it by any means necessary." A lot of people think if you are into some sort of subculture or alternative culture that means you are anti-mainstream. My idea was always "Well, mainstream is kinda sucky a lot of times, but does it have to be?" It would be cool to educate people about the stuff that I'm into. Sort of, enlighten the mainstream—raise the bar all across the board rather than having to feel like an outsider forever.[5]

Geez, Louise. He's right. Too often, I have assumed the wrong motives. **I defaulted to "if they don't think like us, they must be anti-us." A word to myself? Chill.** To other people? Chill. To churches? Chill.

Let people color outside the lines. You just might learn something.

I'll just bet some of you might be struggling with this principle, believing it's your holy responsibility to live "separate from the world" and fix the sin of anybody you come in contact with. Allow me to rattle your cage. In his book, *Lasting Impressions*, Mark Waltz talks about the difference between being responsible to people versus being responsible for them.

We can easily make our approach—our programs, services, classes and groups—more important than the people we want to help. When we do, people feel disrespected, insulted and parented. We are not responsible for people but to them. Being responsible TO our people is quite different. And incredibly freeing.

- When I'm responsible to people, I understand they have a choice. When I'm responsible for people, I think I should decide for them.

- When I'm responsible to people, I know they must figure out their next step. When I'm responsible for people, I try to tell them what their next step is.

- When I'm responsible to people, I allow them to bear the brunt of the consequences for their own chosen actions. When I'm responsible for people, I assume the guilt, or worse the shame, for them.

- When I'm responsible to people, I engage in their journey, offering encouragement and teaching. When I'm responsible for people I try to direct their journey, never allowing them to wrestle, mess up or make a wrong turn.

- When I'm responsible to people, I talk to God on their behalf. When I'm responsible for people, I talk to people a lot on God's behalf.[6]

———————————— •ₒ●● ————————————

You don't have all the answers, so you can quit operating as if you do. Someone might find the courage to take his or her next step toward Christ because you get out of the way.

HOW FAR WOULD YOU GO TO SEE THROUGH THE EYES OF YOUR GUEST?

You get it, by now. We're talking about spending lots of time getting to know the people you're trying to reach. But, here's the kicker. Your job is never done because you can never learn enough about them. Your audience keeps changing.

I attended a conference way back in August 2004. At the end, I was moved, and I wrote this prayer in my notes:

> *Jesus, please don't let the fire in my mission die. Keep me close to the flames and keep me bothered. Don't let me lose touch with real life and real people. Show me people's hearts and pain, so I remember the stakes are high.*

Prayer answered then and still being answered today. Now, I'm consumed by finding new ways to adjust my perspective to see through the eyes of other people. And, I'm challenged daily about how far I would go to understand the reality of their worldview. I'm even discovering new ways to see through the eyes of my co-workers, extended family and enemies. It really is an exercise in dying to yourself. And, for the record, I in no way, shape, or form have it mastered. (But, I am in a constant state of pursuit, just in case you were wondering.)

I'm inspired by the lengths the Walt Disney Corporation takes to do this:

- Disney Imagineers have gone as far as wearing knee-pads* and crawling around their parks to experience them from a child's perspective.

- Every Disney employee is trained in the art of "guestology"—learning who the guests are and what

* Sissies.

they expect when they come to visit. It's a standard part of every employee's job.

- Disney guest services teams set up incognito "listening posts" all around the parks to capture candid feedback about guest impressions.[7]

Why aren't these standard practices for the church? They should be!

We should care about what guests say about us—not just the positives, but the negatives as well (denial is not a good strategy). But, you know the funny thing about negativity? We get the chance to turn it into a positive.[*]

It's probably not practical for me to ask you to go crawl around your lobby wearing kneepads tomorrow, but there are some practical places you can get started to get to know your audience. The more you know about your guests, the better you can communicate with them.[**]

- **Research online chatter.** Use Google, Twitter or Technorati to search[***] your church and pastor's name to see what results you find. You might discover what people say about you when you're not around. Browse the site stuffchristianslike.blogspot.com to see "churchy" habits in a completely new light.

- **Enlist secret shoppers.** Invite people who don't attend church to visit a service or an event or read your bulletin and offer their candid reactions. People love to give their opinion, especially when there are no strings

---

[*] Funny, isn't that what God does for us every day? Ironic.
[**] A big part of this list was inspired by a post I read on ChurchMarketingSucks.com by my friend Brad. If you haven't visited his site yet, you're missing out. His mission? "To frustrate, educate and motivate the church to communicate, with uncompromising clarity, the truth of Jesus Christ." That's gutsy. I dare you to go there now.
[***] Google.com, search.twitter.com and technorati.com.

attached. I heard of one church that had an atheist come to review their service on his blog. I love that.

- **Take surveys.** Use formal and informal polls to see what people are thinking and get feedback about what they believe works and what doesn't. Use different vehicles—bulletin stub, service card, web polls— for a variety of responses.

- **Join them.** Watch the shows people are talking about. Eat where they eat. Read what they read. The more you understand their life, the more you know how to connect with it.

- **Watch them.** Instead of doing what they do, observe how they interact with what they do. Tag along with someone for a day. See what makes them cry, what makes them laugh. What scares them? What moves them to action?

- **Round it out with the demographics.** It's the rest of the story. It doesn't show the whole picture, but including the demographic information in your audience profile is important. The best part is someone else has most likely already done the research for you and you can get it free.*

And, when you're done with all your learnings, then what? Document them and keep them in front of you. Share the summary with your writers, designers, communicators and key leaders to keep in mind as they do their daily jobs. **Without that constant reminder of the bigger picture, it's too easy to fall back to creating your task list and materials for whoever is in front of you—** not necessarily the audience you're trying to reach. Many times, they're not the same.

---

* Looking for places you can get free market research? Go to the "back of the book."

THINK IT OVER

Adopting the best practice—know your audience.

- ☐ How am I defining culture? Do my priorities, actions and decisions help the church "to build," "to care for," "to plant," or "to cultivate"? Or, am I living out the definition as "the way we do things around here"?

- ☐ Am I finding ways to become an amateur ethnographer? What are people rallying around and connecting with? Am I there? Am I finding ways to speak to the need?

- ☐ What new things am I willing to do to step outside my comfort zone to learn about people who don't see things the way I do?

- ☐ If relationships are built on trust, then no one sells better than a peer does. Who are my audience members most like? Who would they rather hear this from than me? How many other people, similar to them, have already gone down this path? What role could they play?

- ☐ How can I promote and perfect the art of "guestology" in my ministry? How will it impact my role, department and task list?

- ☐ Is the audience we're currently reaching the same audience we want to reach? Do we know the difference?

chapter 7

REMOVE BARRIERS TO ENTRY

Distractions are roadblocks and can blind an audience before they ever get the chance to hear or see what's next. Potential distractions exist all around you—from sights, sounds and smells to facilities, signage, preconceived notions, language, graphics and information flow. Your best defense? Identify the distraction and eliminate it. And, you're going to need help with that because most distractions for others are invisible to you. Much like the elephant in the room, sometimes the best way to remove a barrier is to acknowledge it.

THAT'S JUST GROSS

Have you heard about the Toilet Bowl Restaurant in Taiwan?[1] Yes, I used the words "toilet bowl" and "restaurant" in the same sentence. When I first read about it, I was baffled. A restaurant that decorates, seats people at, and serves food in toilets?

Ewww. Seriously, what's the appeal? I've lost my appetite. I don't get it.

This restaurant seems like a good fit for *Fear Factor* contestant training, but wide appeal? I just don't know that many people who want to eat with their friends in the bathroom.*

Think about your ministry programs. Do you have any toilet bowl opportunities you're promoting? In other words, does your audience "get" you (or do only *you* get you)? **Are you freaking people out or helping them lower defenses?**

The ministry promotions I'm going to share with you now may not be as gross as eating out of a toilet bowl, but they are gross examples of real communications misses.

- Promoting a men's retreat as a place to "go deeper and develop relationships with other men." *Try selling that one to your neighbor. Uh... it's not what it sounds like.*

- Providing postcards that have "share this with your unchurched friend" printed on them to your

---

* Believe it or not, they're so successful, they've expanded to multiple locations. However, consider this restaurant an exception to the rule, and don't use it as a model for your ministry.

congregation to use as invites for people they know who don't come to church. *Talk about feeling targeted. What an awkward feeling for the "unchurched friend" when they read that. Are they a person or a project?*

- Asking a newcomer to stand up to be recognized in the service. *This embarrassing moment commonly brought to you by many well-meaning local churches.*

- Using words such as "commitment" and "challenge" in the content of your promotional pieces (e.g., your bulletin or welcome packet). *I'm already overchallenged, overcommitted and overwhelmed. More commitment? My first impression? I don't think I can take it.*

- Jumping in someone's path to shake his or her hand and make them feel welcome at church. *There is such a thing as personal space. I'm glad you noticed I'm here, but not glad to feel assaulted.*

- Use a picture of people holding hands in a circle with their eyes closed to promote small groups. *I'm not sure that's what attracts me to go to someone's house to meet with total strangers. You want me to join a small group and hold hands with total strangers? Try a more inviting first impression.*

The examples here just might have created some barriers for people. Wouldn't you agree?

GET OUT OF YOUR OWN WAY

Just this past year, a friend of mine took a tour of a church with dwindling numbers who was looking for help getting the word out to turn things around. Here's an excerpt from the email he sent me about his experience.

Their Goals

1. They want to attract younger people to the church.

2. They want to create a newer, fresher image and use it to cultivate awareness of their church.

Their Barriers to Entry

1. The median age of the members is 70 years old.

2. Commemorative plaques were located throughout the building dedicating every upgrade to the church (e.g., parking lot paving, welcome center, foyer decor, etc.) to the memory of someone who had died.

3. About 40 really big boxes of Kleenex were located under every pew just inside the aisle. As you walked in they really stood out.

4. A wall of photos in the baby room dated back to the 1930s. The faces of the people were circled with a number next to their face. No explanation about the circles and numbering system existed.

5. The fellowship hall smelled like the inside of a moldy hope chest.

6. A large, framed artist's rendering of what the building would look like after a major stewardship program dated 2001. The campaign was abandoned, but the picture remained in a prominent location.

7. An old-fashioned church attendance reporting sign hung by the "Welcome Center" boasting 55 members in attendance, 33 in Sunday School and an offering of $500.

8. The building was made of cinder blocks painted white with a brown roof and surrounded by a weedy lawn. The only color on the entire property was a tombstone-like plaque in a garden dated 1998.

When the leaders introduced ideas to make their environment inviting to others, they faced resistance from existing members. Somewhere—somehow—these things became sacred and changing them was as unthinkable as desecrating someone's grave.

How sad is it that this reality plays out repeatedly as the things we are used to become more important than the goal of reaching our original objectives? Remember your first love. God called you for a worthy reason, and that reason is not included in any of the eight things listed here.

The right thing to do is simple, although it is rarely easy. Whether you are a pastor, church leader, or ministry servant, do not fear the wrath of the members. Instead, fear the thought of people who will live an eternity without experiencing Christ. Sometimes, you'll experience loss for a short while when you make the right change for the right reason. It is worth it.*

---

* But, don't bull ahead until you finish part three of the book: the responsibility of buy-in.

HOW DARE THOU?

Have you ever been around someone from a specialized industry speaking fluently in technical jargon as you sit there with a big question mark in the thought bubble above your head? I don't know why groups default to these little lexicons of unique jargon only understood and appreciated by their members. It's hard to sift through a steady stream of information without interpretation.

- Do we have an SME who works on this?

- I'm taking a VFR Approach to MHTG.

- Look at your P2P traffic.*

Let's shift gears. What about you? Have you been living a Christian life for a while? You might be speaking "Christianese"—a language that feels so normal to you but leaves others confused. You might need an intervention if you talk like this:**

- How are you? "Blessed."

- How is everything right now? "I'm just trying to let go and let God."

- Why do you like your church? "It helps me with my daily walk."

- Thanks for inviting me today. "The Lord placed it on my heart to witness."

---

*   For those of you going crazy and who are about to put down this book to go look up what these cryptic acronyms mean…let me save you the trouble.
  - SME = Subject Matter Expert. (Corporate-speak)
  - VFR Approach to MHTG = Visual Flight Rules to Tegucigalpa-Toncontin International Airport. (Aviation-speak)
  - P2P = Peer to Peer. (Geek-speak)
** Much thanks to Kathy Guy, Director of Community at Granger Community Church, for helping with this list. She inspired me with a post on her blog becauserelationshipsmatter.net.

- Why do you volunteer? "I feel a burden for the lost."

- How can I get my family to get along? "Just pray."

I have good news. It is possible for you to talk like a normal person again. But, only if you're willing to give up clichés.

Say it with me now: **"The first step is to admit I have a problem. I confess I might be speaking a language that creates an exclusive and intimidating environment.** Sometimes, I use words just to feel a sense of belonging, identity and maybe even superiority over others."

I'm proud of you!

At Granger, we're regularly evaluating our language in the context of the guest perspective. Recognizing that regular people are consumed with the pressures of life (i.e., loneliness, sadness, fear, skepticism, pride, guilt and anger), their filter is set to cope or comprehend based on their "every day." Here are a few words we identified "inside our walls" that needed to change to help improve the way things translate "outside our walls."

Say this:	Instead of this:
• Connection	• Intimacy
• Group	• Small group
• Volunteer	• Fellowship
• Team	• Committee
• Community	• Ministry
• Guest	• Target audience, unchurched and visitor
• Volunteer expo	• Ministry Fair
• Next step	• Go deeper
• Invite	• Recruit
• Opportunity	• Need or help
• Experience	• Attend
• Explore	• Commit
• Growth	• Maturity
• Outreach	• Mission

Mark Twain said,

"The difference between the right word and the almost right word is the difference between lightning and the lightning bug."

What are a few small changes you can make to communicate more effectively in a way that resonates with guests?

MISSION STATEMENT MAD-LIBS

George Bernard Shaw said, "The problem with communication is the illusion that it has been accomplished." Why, then, do people use important words and complex sentence structures to sound more impressive?

Matt Lindeman from 37signals, a software company known for saying "goodbye to bloat," shared this about the sentence structure in an email he received.

"[Redacted] creates the conditions for experimentation and quantitative understanding of the impact of novel management practices in large companies."

The sentence is structured like this: "We create _____ for _____ and _____ of _____ of _____ in _____." It's tough to have anything make sense within that structure.[3]

Can you say "mumbo jumbo"? It made me think of the hazard of mission statements. Look at yours. What about the verbiage you use on your "about us" page? It doesn't sound like the beginning of this email, does it? If it does—priority one—change it!

I used to work for a company where EVERYTHING we produced was written like that. I remember asking about it once, and an executive told me "We're dealing with quants* here. They won't take us seriously if we don't sound as smart as them. It's what they're looking for."**

Ayyy, yi, yi. [Shudder.] It has taken me years to unlearn that phantom logic. Ridiculousness. Crazy talk. Stop the madness.

---

* In the investment industry, people who perform quantitative analysis are called quants.
** No liberties were taken with this example for dramatic effect. It was a verbatim quote from a very smart man I used to work with. While he was very successful and easily pulled in a six-figure annual income, I'm not convinced this was a very smart statement.

THEMING A CAPITAL CAMPAIGN

Every one of us has the tendency to turn inward unless we're reminded to turn outward. It's human nature to default to "It's all about me." So, instead of fighting it, we just went with it and themed our last capital campaign "My Life."

BELONGING. CHANGING. SHARING.

At first, this might seem like a contradiction to the desired spiritual growth we're teaching about (i.e., "it's not about me"). But, see if this three-part rationale doesn't help connect the dots.

1. **Until somebody owns it, he or she is not likely to go the extra mile.** Regardless of age, environment, or spiritual health, there's an immediate connection and sense of ownership when "it's all about me." You can get a lot of mileage out of it; it's *my* story, it's *my* decision, it's *my* chance to make a difference, it's *my* place, *my* space, *my* life. I own it.

2. **It's a multi-dimensional message: Belonging. Changing. Sharing.** The tagline projects movement and addresses all parts of the journey—personal, church, and community. It progressively moves from felt-need to action.

3. **It's believable.** It's personal and doesn't sound like a national sales convention or fundraiser. It creates possibilities.

4. **It's simple.** Short and to the point, it's easy to remember and easy to use in creative story telling.

Ah, there it is. The stories—in print, video, on the web and live from the platform. It's in those stories of changed lives where people get inspired and shift their thinking from self to others.

I heard Erwin McMannus speak at a conference recently where he described the "first space" as the space where we engage with people *who like me* because they *are like me* and the "second space" as the place you earn the right to be heard and interact with others. **If we don't create a first space in the church, people will never experience the church in the second-space moments of their world.**

MICKEY'S TEN COMMANDMENTS

In the book, *Be Our Guest*, Walt Disney's Vice Chairman Marty Sklar shared the list of design principles he created for how Disney delivers its service themes and standards. He said he created the list from what he learned from his principal mentors Walt Disney and John Hench.

Think about your church as you read his list. Think about the individual ministries and departments. Think about your brochures, your Web site, your lobby, your postcards, your email—every touchpoint that a guest experiences. Ready?

1. **Know your audience.** Before creating a setting, obtain a firm understanding of who will be using it.

2. **Wear your guest's shoes.** That is, never forget the human factor. Evaluate your setting from the customer's perspective by experiencing it as a customer.

3. **Organize the flow of people and ideas.** Think of a setting as a story and tell that story in a sequenced, organized way. Build the same order and logic into the design of customer movement.

4. **Create a visual magnet.** It's a visual landmark used to orient and attract people.

5. **Communicate with visual literacy.** Language is not always composed of words. Use common languages of color, shape and form to communicate through a setting.

6. **Avoid overload—create turn-ons.** Do not bombard customers with data. Let them choose the information they want when they want it.

7. **Tell one story at a time.** Mixing multiple stories in a single setting is confusing. Create one setting for each big idea.

8. **Avoid contradictions; maintain identity.** Every detail and every setting should support and further your organizational identity and mission.

9. **For every ounce of treatment, provide a ton of treat.** Give your customers the highest value by building an interactive setting that gives them the opportunity to exercise all of their senses.

10. **Keep it up.** Never get complacent, and always maintain your setting.[4]

And, there you have it. The keys to the Magic Kingdom. Ten ways Walt Disney harnessed the talents and hearts of his "cast members" with one vision to create unparalleled entertainment experiences. If it works for a mouse, why aren't more churches following these commandments?

THINK IT OVER

Adopting the best practice—remove barriers to entry.

- ☐ What are a few small changes we can make to our organizational language to communicate more effectively in a way that resonates with more people? Are we consistent with the language we use in all of our media (e.g., messages, bulletins, newsletters, signage, events, etc.)?

- ☐ Am I focusing on my content over communication? What information is not being presented for interpretation?

- ☐ How can I uncover the barriers to entry that are invisible to me in our environment? Once identified, am I prepared to make a change?

- ☐ Where am I fearful to change because of the resistance I'll experience from the regulars or staffers stuck in a rut? How can I avoid a classic case of misplaced priorities?

- ☐ At the end of the day, am I taking down roadblocks between our guests and God? Am I the roadblock? What do I need to unlearn?

- ☐ What do my guests see, hear, smell and feel in our environment? Does it attract or repel?

chapter 8
REDUCE THE NOISE

People are stressed out, fed up, over committed (in time and money), and over stimulated. Under any kind of stress (i.e., traffic, deadline, crying kids, finances), the loudest signals your brain sends out are about what's happening right at this moment and how to survive it. Anything that's not critical to this moment physiologically is drowned out. It's how God has designed the human brain to prioritize. People need inspiration first, so the information will sink in. Many times that inspiration will come from how you make them feel, not by what you have to say. People argue, "It doesn't matter how we make people feel; our job isn't to make them feel good. Our job is to tell the truth in love." *Does it matter how people feel?* If your goal is effective communication, then, yes, it matters immensely. A person needs to be reachable before they're teachable.

YOU GOT FAMILIES IN YOUR CHURCH?

If you have families in your church, I wonder if you know what they're dealing with outside the church walls.

I'll use my friend Michelle as just one example. She has two girls in school—one in third grade and one in fourth grade. Just five days into the school year, the girls had brought home over 100 pieces of paper. One hundred pieces of paper in five days. For two children. Just two.

From Michelle Wegner's blog.[1]

There is something terribly wrong here. How many weeks of school are there? After one month, her two girls had brought home over 200 pieces of paper between them. Michelle asked, "Can you help me figure out what is important and what I should keep? I went to college, and I can't figure it out."

I happen to have two kids of my own still in school, and I can relate. It takes me 10 to 20 minutes to sort through the handouts and flyers sent home with them every day. It stresses me out. I'm trying to live my life, and it feels like someone else is taking control of my time and my kitchen counter by overwhelming me with clutter. I seriously don't have the time or patience to figure out what they say is important, especially when they communicate that *everything* is important.

You might be asking yourself "why is she telling me this?" You might catch yourself thinking, "Look, missy, your issue is not my issue."

Well, maybe. And, maybe not. Before you create that mass mailing, hand out that brochure, or send that email,* ask yourself,

> **"Will this information I intend to be helpful just add to the clutter?"**

If you can't be sure, go farther.

> **"Is there any way to simplify what my audience sees to make their experience with the church easier and more rewarding?"**

Because, Lord knows, the public school system isn't asking themselves these questions. It's the least we can do as the Church. Don't you think?

---

* In November 2008, our spam filter caught more than 183,000 incoming messages. Can you tell me why your email is any different than the other 183,000?

PARK'S A KILLER

My friend Tim works at Park Community Church in Chicago and, in the summer of 2008, they killed their weekly bulletin. Whoa. Bold move. But, smart.

Park went into the decision to kill the weekly bulletin strategically. I think their solution—the monthly bulletin—is a win in their setting.

Here's why it makes sense for us.

1. **We are a young church.** Not young in the sense of how long we've been around (20 years), but in the sense of our average age. It's 29.

2. **We are a "mobile" church.** Our people work in the Loop, live by their smart phones, are single, on Facebook, texting and Twittering.

3. **Our content was stagnant.** On any given week we were just shuffling around the same information in our programs, maybe adding only 1 or 2 new things.

4. **Uh, hello.** Every week we threw away scores of bulletins people left behind. It was crazy.

The pros of our choice.

1. **Budget savings.** We cut our monthly printing budget by 75%.

2. **Environmental savings.** We're not killing as many trees. It's a "green" choice the people in our church rally behind.

3. **Smart resourcing.** It forced our organization to plan out events in advance instead of waiting to the last minute. This was our old mode of operation.

4. **Focus.** It forced us to prioritize and condense. We went from thoughtlessly publishing everything, to choosing only to publish the things that would further the mission and vision of our church. And, what we do decide to communicate has to be done in a few sentences, not an entire paragraph.[*2]

Even if we decide it makes sense to let our weekly bulletin live, there are interesting points Tim highlights about their decision we all should at least consider.

* You can read more about Park's communication revolution on Tim's blog: timschraeder.typepad.com.

WHO MAKES THE CALL?

If I had a dollar for every time someone asked me, "When somebody wants something advertised, who decides how and where it gets promoted?" I could probably buy myself something significant, like a co-pay for a pediatrician visit or something else that costs around $50.

The question shouldn't be "who decides it?" but "what drives it?" At Granger, we've put some systems in place to make it easy to get the word out and find it once it's out there. In an effort to reduce the noise for our people, we* started by documenting two things to help us define "what drives it."

1. **Our communication values.** A list of attributes about how we communicate and how we don't.

2. **Our communication priorities.** A list of our promotion categories and sample deliverables.**

When you decide *in advance* how and what you communicate as an organization, you don't have to figure it out repeatedly with each individual request. The following guidelines create the systems that help reduce noise for both our internal and external audiences. They remove subjectivity and "make the call" for us 90% of the time.

- **Prioritize based on scope.** Because we recognize everything may be important, not everything is EQUALLY important and appropriate for "all church" consumption. When you treat everything the same, it gets noisy. Depending on the amount of people it affects, items fall into one of the following categories.

---

* Who is "we"? I wrote the first draft with my communication team for my senior management team to react to. They had the chance to edit and correct before signing off on the final copy but didn't have to write the entire thing from scratch.
** You can find a sample of both documents in "the back of the book."

Each category has typical deliverables associated with it.

- *Heavy emphasis.* The 20% of what's happening that affects 80% of the audience—this week in the main auditorium, next steps out of the weekend, and all-church events.

- *Medium emphasis.* Mid-sized events that affect a larger group, but not 80% of the audience.

- *Light emphasis.* Niche news, team meetings or small volume events.

- **Invest minimal resources into print materials.** We don't attempt to go for the "sell" with ministry or event brochures. We invest that energy into personal invites and the event experience. Why? Print materials have a limited shelf life (especially with the pace of ministry and volunteers), create a lot of production activity and cost with little return and add to the clutter. When we do need print materials for events, we skip the elaborate design and marketing copy to focus on the basic: who, what, where and when. When is the last time you made a decision to purchase something because of direct mail advertising?

- **Identify one place to keep all information up-to-date.** Our Web site is where we update all news in one place that's accessible by everyone. It doesn't matter what your role is (e.g., staff, volunteer or attendee) or what question you have—everybody knows the one place to go for the answer. We don't have to create special materials for our guest services desk because they use the Web site, too. If a guest needs a handout, they print it from the Web site. And, what about our

bulletin and enewsletter? Same thing. We don't duplicate in them what's on the Web. We use them as tools
to create awareness and drive people back to the Web
site for the rest of the details. For you, the *one* place
may not be the Web. Whatever you choose, stick with
that one place, and drive everyone back to it.

GET REAL

I already talked about 37signals earlier in chapter seven, and I'm going to talk about them again. I can't help it. They set the bar for corporate self-control, and they are making the world a better place because of it.* They published a free online book called *Getting Real* that's all about how they do successful projects by keeping things simple. It starts with their modus operandi:

We believe software is too complex. Too many features, too many buttons, too much to learn. Our products do less than the competition—intentionally. We build products that work smarter, feel better, allow you to do things your way and are easier to use.[3]

That is beautiful. Somebody hand me a tissue. No, I'm serious. Their book is not a rant about technology and project management. It has broad principles that apply to all of mankind.** Look at the transferable principles I found in their introduction alone!

What Is *Getting Real*?

- Getting Real is about skipping all the stuff that represents real and actually building the real thing.

- Getting Real is less. Less mass, less software, less features, less paperwork, less of everything that's not essential (and most of what you think is essential actually isn't).

---

* Sense the personal bias? No! None whatsoever.
** Am I being too dramatic? I think not.

- Getting Real is staying small and being agile.

- Getting Real starts with what the customer actually experiences and builds backwards from there. This lets you get it right before you get it wrong.

- Getting Real delivers just what customers need and eliminates anything they don't.

We used these bullets as talking points for a web team brainstorm we had earlier this year.

The result was like virtual liposuction.

- We identified how bloated our site had become. After adding so many pages over the years, people had stopped reading them. If they're not helping—they need to go.

- We changed our menu structure. Instead of fat navigation with choices organized like a research paper outline, we slimmed it down and added action-oriented links. In other words, instead of trying to figure out what needed to be said, we figured out what tasks people were trying to get done.

- We took the suit off our site and dressed it in khakis. Instead of creating sterilized content, we gave people links to real-time content and conversations (i.e., select blogs,[*] Twitter feeds, Facebook pages, etc.).[**]

---

[*] We don't link to everybody that blogs on staff or the list would never end. We highlight a few leader and team blogs.

[**] I've seen sites dressed in jeans. They are very casual, very organic, very free-form. I love some of those sites. We didn't go that far because it wasn't consistent with our corporate personality. But, neither was the suit. The khakis were just right for us.

- We found ways to give people access to stuff they wanted, instead of creating more pages for the stuff we thought they needed. For example, we improved our search feature and made it more visible. We started posting more media elements from our weekend services for people to watch again and share with their friends.

Who knew that a nip/tuck could be the smartest thing for a church to do? It's worth setting aside the time to ask yourself how to get real instead of trying so hard to appear real.

FREQUENCY COULD ADD TO THE CLUTTER

A common pillar of advice you will find about blogging will tell you that post frequency is the secret to blog success. People say the more often you publish on your blog, the higher your readership will be. I've been writing for my blog since 2005, and I never agreed with that advice. Not every blog needs to deliver a daily dose of wisdom or hot news.

My opinion was finally affirmed when I read an article by Eric Kintz, a marketing executive at Hewlett-Packard. In an instant, I went from blog hack to strategic blogging genius. From zero to hero. Eric said post frequency doesn't matter as it did in the early blogging days. And, here's why:

- The blogosphere doubles in size every six months, and cutting through the clutter is more difficult with daily posts.

- Traffic doesn't make a blog successful—engaging your audience (which may be narrow and focused) does.

- Loyal readers remain loyal because they subscribe to your blog, not because you post frequently.

- The pressure of frequent posting has the potential to drive poor content quality.

- Frequent posting could push corporate bloggers into the hands of PR agencies. That decreases authenticity and creditability.[4]

If you ever feel the pressure to post daily or weekly, I'm here to tell you to breathe easy. As an individual, I give you permission to blog in spurts when you're inspired. As an organization, blog only when you have something worthy to add. For a church, I would guess you'd have something new of value at least once a week.

For a company, it could be a couple of times a month. The point? **Don't let frequency become your objective. Make sure you have something uniquely helpful you're bringing to the table before you hit "publish" on that blog (or "send" for that enews).**

PLEASE DON'T MAKE ME WORK SO HARD

You know what it feels like to get a long-winded letter or email from someone that exhausts or frustrates you the minute you open it, you know, when you're bombarded with tiny words, run-on sentences, single-spaced lines or volume without context—the experience is underwhelming at best, and at worst, you're frustrated at the time it takes out of your life without adding back value in return.*

To find the value in content such as that, you're forced to take the time to sort through the overgrown mass because the author didn't take the time before sending it. But, who has that luxury? I know I don't. I don't have the time to do someone's work for them.

Well, ok, just this one time. Let's use this email my friend got from her insurance company as a case study.

Before:

> Dear UnumProvident Customer:
>
> A lot has changed over the last several years, and in many respects we are a new company today—one that is better positioned to capitalize on the tremendous opportunities that lie ahead. One of our goals for 2007, in addition to continuing to build on the momentum we've established, is to enhance the marketing of our products and services. With this in mind, we have been undertaking a complete brand review with the intention of developing a new brand identity that better leverages our unique strengths in the marketplace.

---

* I rambled on and on in the first paragraph to prove a point. It wasn't a good experience for you, was it? See what I mean?

As a first step in what will be some exciting changes to our brand, I'm pleased to announce today that we are changing our name to **Unum**. The name is intended to simplify the brand, without losing sight of the valuable brand equity we've built in the marketplace over many years. In addition to having strong awareness among customers and brokers, the name Unum also provides a better fit as we focus more of our efforts on being a leader in benefits sold to and through the workplace. In many respects, this action is simply formalizing what many of you have already been doing—abbreviating our name to Unum.

The names attached to the legal insurance entities we use to market our products, such as Unum Life Insurance Company of America, provident Life & Accident Insurance Company, The Paul Revere Life Insurance Company, and Colonial Life & Accident Insurance Company, will remain the same. We plan to share more with you on our branding initiatives, including a new corporate logo, later this spring. In the meantime, the correspondence you receive from us many still carry the UnumProvident name, as we phase in our new name.

Thank you for your continued support of our company. We value the opportunity to serve your employee benefits needs, and we look forward to a continued partnership between your organization and the new Unum.

Sincerely,

Tom Watjen

President and CEO

Unum is a good company and my friend was a completely satisfied customer. But, when she received this letter, she was left asking, "Huh? *Why* did you send this to me, and *what* am I supposed to do about it?"

What about you? Do you have any idea what they're saying and why we should care? Me, neither. But, I can guess. And, here's how I would rewrite the letter for them. Free of charge.

After:

Dear UnumProvident Customer:

We wanted you to know, we're changing our name to Unum. It's simple—which is probably why many of you are already abbreviating it anyway. We're just following your lead.

The transition will take just a little while to phase into, so you might receive some correspondence from us that still carries the old UnumProvident name.

Thank you for your continued support of our company. We value the opportunity to serve your employee benefits needs.

I'm not picking on Tom (or his staff). Businesses aren't the only ones who talk too much about themselves and forget to filter their message through the eyes of their audience. Churches can be the worst. But, it's not too late to break the cycle. **Say less. Value people's time.**

THINK IT OVER

Adopting the best practice—reduce the noise.

☐ Do I look for ways to alleviate the barrage of information my audience receives from me? Do I proactively look for ways to make it easier to sort and digest, or do I just throw it all up at once, leaving my audience to pick up the pieces?

☐ It's been said that the brain can only absorb what the seat can endure. Am I still talking when my audience's seat is beat?

☐ If I go back and look at what we're putting out there for people to read with new eyes, how much can I cut to value people's time?

☐ What corporate communication are we sending that's babble? What opportunities do we have to get real instead of trying so hard to *appear* real?

☐ What content do we have "just to have it" that is out-of-date, redundant or irrelevant? Churches always seem to have "this is who we are" and "this is what we do" print materials. When was the last time I saw these same types of materials at the post office, the doctor's office, Starbucks or Wal-Mart?

chapter 9
TELL ONE STORY AT A TIME

One thing is more important than all the rest in what you're doing. Do you know what it is? Can you communicate it in one sentence? Theologian Joseph Priestley says, "The more elaborate our means of communication, the less we communicate."[1] If you don't know what that one sentence is, how do you expect other people to figure it out? Each communication piece is a valuable tool with the opportunity to unify all communications or dilute them. How many stories are you telling? Sometimes the secret in finding the right thing to say is in knowing what not to say.

LIVING OUT YOUR STORY ONLINE

Everything you do is an extension of your story. Does your communication strategy consider that at every touchpoint? For example, how would it play out on your Web site? Here's how we do it.

In this era of information overload—and life at light-speed—we strive to provide escape hatches. And, our Web site is one of them. We've designed it to answer the two most important questions:

1. Is this a fit for me?

2. If so, what is my next step?

What you won't find on the site is the snack menu for the toddler room. Because people just need to know when that room is staffed and ready for their child. And, they don't need a page on the philosophy of our men's ministry—but a story of life-change from other men who attend Granger. Am I right?

What you *will* find:

- **Who we are**—the story, the staff, the philosophy and a slice of the Granger Community Church experience.

- **Where we are**—who and what happens at our two campuses and community center.

- **Things to do**—links to where you can get help, get involved, and get connected to other people at Granger.

THE IMPORTANCE OF FLOW

One definition of flow is "to move or run smoothly with unbroken continuity." In other words, people shouldn't notice the process. If they do, it's broken.

What roadblocks get in the way of what people are trying to do in your church? There are plenty of areas to evaluate flow, and here are some places to start.

- **Eliminate the extra steps.** Don't make people "call for more information." Anticipate the basic questions they will ask, and give them a direct channel to show up, register or RSVP. If you're using this as your "connection point," I recommend you revisit that strategy. I love it when my doctor calls to remind me of an upcoming appointment. But, I hate it when they leave multiple messages asking me to call to confirm. Instead of "call [so & so] for more information," how about just giving the information people need up front? The basic who, what, when, where and how works almost every time. If I want to talk to someone, I can. But, don't make me.

- **Eliminate confusing treasure hunts.** Think of how people experience and navigate in a department store. The inventory is constantly changing, but the departments are constant. I know what direction to head, no matter what I'm looking for, and there are multiple ways to get there. At Granger, we've identified four pages on our site where you can find anything that's happening: home, events, volunteer or group. By doing this, we have more time to focus on creating experiences and relationships in our teams and events, not by creating more content. And, the best part is people don't get lost on our site.

- **Eliminate assumptions.** Don't assume your audience will train themselves. They won't. Don't assume people wake up in the morning and check the church Web site. They don't. Don't assume people will tell you when a process or link is broken. They probably won't. Don't assume the parents don't read the student ministry blog. They do, whether you're talking to them or not.

- **Eliminate extra work for people.** Instead of organizing your staff directory by name and title, how about arranging it alphabetically by frequently asked questions or by subject? Make it easy to find the right person by topic versus title.

The benefit of paying close attention to flow is a great experience. When everything flows naturally, your guests have a lasting impression of a place where the actions match the words, and the result is a trustworthy environment across departments and media. **When you break flow, you risk surprising people with conflicting personalities in the same experience.** That's frustrating to people, and it's not the story you want them to leave with and tell their friends.

YOU CAN'T SAY EVERYTHING AT ONCE

How many verbal announcements are appropriate from the platform? Research shows that after two announcements, people generally stop listening. But, even when we know the answer, churches still struggle when service time comes around. We believe there are so many important things that "have to be said" during the service, we just can't control ourselves. We think if we don't say it, people won't hear it. Well, they're not hearing it anyway.

Allow me to share a story that comes at it from a different angle. No matter how many times I was told, nobody could convince me it was worth the extra time to cut the plastic ring from the milk jug before I threw it away. I wasn't convinced it would make a difference for "the benefit of the environment," the constant reminders were annoying, and I tuned out every time. That is, until my kids showed me the picture of the poor deformed turtle. You know the one I'm talking about—the turtle that swam through a milk jug ring?

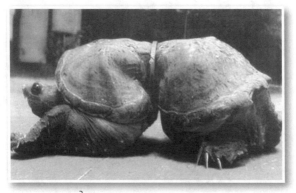

Poor little turtle.[2]

And, that's all it took. I will not be responsible for disfiguring a poor, little, defenseless turtle who was swimming along minding his own business when—in an instant—his life's potential was cut short. Now I never throw away those little plastic rings without cutting them in half first.

Sometimes it takes just the right image for us to "get it." Well, we can thank my mom for emailing me this next photo. When I saw it, I immediately thought of what happens when we try to say everything at once.

Force feeding. It doesn't end well.

May this image be forever burned in your head as the little turtle image is burned in mine. Call it to mind to help remember to tell one story at a time. When you mix multiple stories in a single setting (e.g., meeting, service, Web site, brochure, letter), it blocks the message. Create one setting for each big idea.*

* If you must tell more than one story at a time, may I suggest you carpool? Try to tie multiple messages together into one cohesive thought. Group them. Theme them. Carpool.

LESSONS FROM LUCKY

Here's a little blast from my past I'm going to share with you. I pulled it off my blog (the closest thing I have to a journal these days).

- Today, January 12, 2006, I was almost killed by a vicious animal. I have the giant paw prints and witnesses to prove it.

- I was able to run for my flippin' life and make it into the house in time. Miracles do still happen.

- In the face of death, somehow I didn't pee my pants. This is truly amazing.

- I met my new neighbor for the first time when I called the police on her dog. Awkward.

- She tells me "Lucky" just needs to get to know me and that I need to come over to meet him. Uh, excuse me, are you high?

- The president of the homeowner's association stopped by to welcome me to the neighborhood. And, to find out why I had the street lined with emergency vehicles.

- I didn't feel very lucky when "Lucky", the 110-pound Rottweiler, was running directly at me, full speed, eyes locked, teeth bared, drool flowing, growl gurgling.

Days later, when I was over the trauma, I started reflecting on the "disconnect" Lucky created for the story his owner was telling me. She went on and on and on about how "Lucky isn't usually like this." Her mouth was moving, but the picture of the maniacal, ferocious killer in my head that I had experienced just moments before was speaking louder. She continued, "He's so gentle and protective over the kids. He's usually so sweet. This is highly unusual."

This is what I hear, "Blah. Blah. Blah. Blah. Blah." Nothing she can do or say will erase the story I have in my mind. "I'll have you over to share a bottle of wine." Nope. Your dog is still psychotic and dangerous, and I'm afraid to let my kids go in the backyard until he is gone or put on Prozac. Believe what you want, dog owner blinded by love. My reality is defined by my experience with Lucky, and it doesn't match yours.

The same is true in our ministry environments. People leave with the "actual" experience, and that's what they talk about. They don't leave with our intentions or what we are "usually like." If we make one person feel unwelcome, forget to return a phone call, mess up registration because of disorganization—that's all they remember.

Sweat the details. Stay "on" at all times, and go out of your way to make positive first impressions—in your communications, your personal interactions and your organization. Think about the guest over the organization at all times. It's their perspective that matters first. It's hard to recover from a negative impression because, many times, people are gone before you even know you've messed up.

Things happen. So, when they do (and you know about it), own them. Apologize. Undo the perceived injustice. It's a great opportunity to turn that negative into a positive. Don't make excuses for Lucky. Just apologize for him attacking me.

THREE EASY WAYS TO LOSE YOUR IDENTITY

Your *identity* is your brand. Not your logo. Not your design. Not your programs. However, you *live out* your identity through your logo, your design, your programs, etc. A common thread needs to string through everything you do to avoid committing brand suicide. One thread.

Jeremy Scheller is the "head honcho of a department of one" at the Sanctuary Church in Minneapolis. On the side, he's part of a two-person creative agency designed to help people enjoy a positive brand experience. I like to hear his thoughts from time to time because he calls it as he sees it. In his typical style, he shares three easy ways to lose your identity. [3]

1. **Have too many of them.** Not everything in your organization needs a name, logo and stylesheet all to itself. When you overbrand, you dilute your core message. When everything has its own identity, you end up competing with yourself. It's like *Fight Club* all over again.

2. **Borrow it from someone else.** It's easy to get inspired by design. Some things are just drop-dead beautiful. But, it's hard to be yourself if you're trying to be somebody else. Be inspired, but don't imitate.

3. **Sparkle without substance.** If you oversell yourself, eventually, people will figure you out. You can only fool people for so long. A candy coated Brussels sprout isn't going to hide the bitter taste when you bite into the core.

Andy Sernovitz, author of the book *Word of Mouth Marketing: How Smart Companies Get People Talking,* is clear about it,

> **"There is no 'and' in brand. A great brand can only be one thing. You can't sell yourself as fastest and smartest—people don't know how to process those conflicting ideas. Here's the test: Say what you do out loud. Is there an 'and' in there? If yes, you lose."[4]**

But, you're good at so many things! You're going to change the world! I know. I know. But, what's that one, specific, unique thread weaving through everything I experience at your church? Is it your compassion? Is it your arts? Is it your warmth? Is it your excellence? Is it your international impact? Is it your family focus? One thing, over everything else. That's your identity.

Ours?

> **"Helping people take their next step toward Christ... together."**

One step at a time. The next right thing. No lone rangers. No isolation. This is the common thread, the one thing that permeates everything we do.

YOU'VE BEEN FRAMED

Have you heard of the art of framing? It's the use of words, images and interactions to speak to, or avoid provoking, a bias someone is already feeling. It's how you piece all the parts together—language, images, environment—to tell a story. Framing is learning to communicate by seeing the world through someone else's eyes.

What story does this picture tell you?

It's not what you think.

Without the proper framing, you probably wouldn't know that Mommy works at Lowe's and is selling a snow shovel. How you frame your story matters. What images you use matters. What language you use matters. The context in which you share it matters.

I heard that it's difficult to see the picture when you're inside the frame. How true. How true.

Framing is not the same thing as "spin." As a recovering corporate spin doctor, I'm opinionated about the difference between the two. It's clear to me: **Spin is *selfish* manipulation for personal gain. Framing is *selfless*, requiring you to step out of the frame to look at the whole picture for the benefit of others.**

Mark Batterson, lead pastor of National Community Church in Washington, DC, talks about framing and leadership.

———————————— •●●• ————————————

A good coach knows how to reframe a game at halftime.

A good psychologist knows how to reframe a problem.

A good parent knows how to reframe spinach—the vegetable that will give you bulging biceps like Popeye.

Good leaders are good at putting the right frame around a vision.

Good preachers frame their messages with an organizing metaphor around biblical truths that make people say "I've never thought about it that way before."[5]

———————————— •●●● ————————————

He brings wise context to the subject. **How we frame our message—challenges and opportunities—directly affects how people respond.**

THINK IT OVER

Adopting the best practice—tell one story at a time.

☐ If I evaluate everything that happens at our church as a "story," is it cohesive and comprehensible? Do the environments feel as if they're from the same family, or like a hodgepodge of competing values?

☐ Are competing personalities on our team hurting the story? Am I afraid to deal with staff baggage proactively? How can I diffuse emotion to get people on the same page by encouraging cohesiveness, not cloning?

☐ People hate to be sold, but they love to buy. And, my audience is full of people who don't want to hear about how wonderful we think our product or service is. How can we breathe life into our flat "information" to help people imagine their owning and loving it for themselves? Is it something people will want to attach themselves to?

☐ How many stories are we telling with the amount of information we produce, the quality of each piece, and how we organize the information?

☐ What is the one thread of our identity? Is every ministry telling the same story?

chapter 10

UNTANGLE THE WEB

Bad Web sites happen to good people. I think it's an epidemic. It doesn't matter if you build it, pay for it, are hands-on, hands-off, a web master or web disaster—I'm talking to you. And, I'm going to tell you what you probably won't hear anywhere else. If you want a Web site that works, make paper first. [screeching brakes] That's right. I said, "make paper."* You see, the secret to making Web sites that work is to make the paper that holds the plan for your Web site. That plan replaces the wrong questions with the right ones. The right questions prevent you from falling victim to one-size-fits-none solutions, empty vendor-speak, and technology buzz-babble. Do you want to unleash the power of the Web? Start by asking, "What is the desired response we want" instead of "What do we want this to look like," and work backwards from there.

* Admit it. You think that, after nine chapters, I'm losing my mind.

WHAT IT IS AND WHAT IT ISN'T

Bad Web sites begin with a bad definition. If you don't know what it is, then you're not going to know how to best use it. Am I right? Here's a list that might help reset some filters about what can make, or break, a Web site.

Web sites are...	Web sites are not...
• An extension of what you do	• A stand-alone deliverable
• About communications	• About technology
• Tools that plug people in	• Tools that plug-in to the Web
• A process	• A place
• An experience	• A page
• A place for what you need now	• An archive for everything

When you are able to operate within this new definition, you will be more equipped not only to control better the flow of information, but also the flow of attention. And, here is the best news of all. You don't need a big budget or a big brain to make your Web site work for you (instead of the other way around). All you need to do is ask the right questions in the right context before you decide on your site's content and design. The answers you find in the right frame of mind allow you to make good decisions about what your site does (and doesn't do).

Take off the technology glasses and stop looking at the Web as an online brochure or complicated piece of code. Start looking at it as an environment where people gather and might bring their friends. That changes the rules of the game.

FINISH YOUR BLUEPRINT BEFORE YOU BREAK GROUND

You don't build a house a room at a time. You get the plans for the entire house before you make your shopping list and start hiring contractors. Nobody would look at a skyscraper after it was built and say, "I wonder how we're going to add a garage to that?" A Web site is no different; you need a master plan before you build. Here's a simple framework you can use, with sample questions along the way, to help you start the process of writing your web blueprint.

Phase 1: Discover

Fragmented identity equates to lost identity. That is why the process begins with questions about your organization—not your Web site. Use Phase 1 to *discover* competing values and address them. Everything that touches your audience sends a message. Make sure you know what that message is, so you can positively reinforce the message you want to send—online and off.

- What is our ministry compass, our statement of purpose? What values do we adhere to? What can we offer that can't be found anywhere else?

- What audience are we trying to reach? Is it the same audience we are reaching now?

- What is the information flow for our church? How do events get promoted? Do we have one calendar? One database?

Phase 2: Define

In Phase 1, you got clarity about who you are, what you do and what type of experience you want to create. Phase 2 is where you *define* how you want to tell that story specifically on the Web.

- What audience will we serve first? Who is our secondary audience?

- What are our objectives? What will happen as a result of this new site? How will we measure our success?

- What is our current reality (e.g., budget, staffing, technology platform, etc.)?

- What's working with our current site? What's not working?

These first two phases are the most important, and you should spend the majority of your time and effort here.[*] In them, you find the answers that morph into your project scope—that blueprint you'll use to stay on track and make ongoing decisions. But, depending on what you find, you may need to take some time repairing your infrastructure before moving to Phase 3.

Phase 3: Deliver

By this point in the process, you've probably figured out that you won't be able to do everything you originally set out to do. But, that's ok. Your action plan has clarity—about not only what you're saying no to, but also more importantly, about what you're saying yes to.

- List your deliverables by priorities: now, soon, and later.

- There is more to your project than development. Make sure to leave room for concepts, testing and content.

- Remember, "like a house." Make a plan for

---

[*] I was hired to build a new Web site in 2002. It took two years to find clear answers to the questions in Phases 1 and 2. It took another year for Phase 3. The new site went live in 2005. True story. The point is, this is a process. Don't be tempted to take shortcuts. It will be worth it in the end.

maintenance (bug fixes), improvements (enhancements) and remodeling (upgrades).

Not only does a master plan provide a good outlet for ideas you can't tackle today, it also reminds people what you agreed to do in the first place.* Your finished document will help manage information across multiple departments, establish a unified vision and prevent unnecessary revisions.**

---

* Newsflash: People have short memories and define reality by their emotion of the day. Document everything.
** Obviously, there is more to defining your web strategy than I can outline in these few pages. However, this may be just what you need to get started and turn things around.

DON'T COMPLICATE THE SOLUTION

Enhancing productivity means embracing simplicity.* Many times, we have the power to "simplify real-world problems by defining them to be simple";[1] we just don't use it. Steve Smith, recognized web development and design expert, built an entire company around this concept. He talks about making the complex simple on his blog.

> "One of my favorite quotes is *Simplify the Problem, Don't Complicate the Solution.* Before you attack a complicated, real-world problem with an equally complex solution, step back and see if you can't figure out a way to make the problem simpler to start with. Simple problems make for simple solutions."[2]

Recently, I met with a ministry leader who was under pressure from one of his remote teams for a solution to their current crisis. Their numbers had grown significantly, and they needed help checking kids in at a weekly event.

The only solution they saw was to implement a web portal with check-in kiosks like we use at our Granger campus. The ministry leader entered our conversation a bit discouraged, knowing that while real challenges existed, they didn't have the money to implement the solution they needed. Or, did they?

While their numbers had grown significantly, they were only dealing with 70 adults (30–45 children) at this remote site. But, because they had started with no system at all, this number became overwhelming to manage in a hurry. And, because they saw the kiosk system we use at the Granger campus, they assumed that was the best and only answer.

---

* I think it was Monte Ford, SVP Information Technology and CIO at American Airlines, who gets the credit for saying this first.

I asked a few questions and listened. After I was sure I understood their objective, I "defined the problem to be simple." Even though the conversation started with the need for a web portal, it ended here: associate children with the person who drops them off at check-in (thus ensuring child safety at pick-up).

For years, we had used a paper-sticker system at our church to check in kids and maintain security. We effectively used the same paper-sticker system for 15 years and did not integrate check-in with our Web site until we reached a weekend attendance of more than 4,000 people. That remote team didn't need a web portal after all. They just needed stickers. Simple, cheap and effective.

Keep it simple, it works. Our sticker check-in security system.

My pastor, Mark Beeson, addressed this matter of complexity very well in a strategy meeting our team had earlier this year: "There is something bad about size and complexity. The more complex things are, the more fragile they are. If you have a stone, you can bang it. No problem. As soon as you play mousetrap, if any link in the chain is off, the whole system stops." **Remember, simplify the problem. Don't complicate the solution.**

JUST BECAUSE YOU BUILD IT DOESN'T MEAN THEY'LL COME

Unless your site is an online scrapbook, it's not about you. It's about the person you want to visit the site (and hopefully come back). With your Web site, it is better to focus on the outside more than what's on the inside. Too many Web sites are self-centered or self-absorbed. Consequently, it sends the message that the organization is self-centered and self-absorbed. Is your site self-absorbed?

- Is your site map organized by your organizational chart or ministry list? Consider organizing it around tasks and opportunities instead.

- Do you split long copy into multiple pages? Don't make people scroll; help them scan. Give them more bullets and fewer clicks.

- Do you have an "under construction" page? Don't tell people to check back, just turn it on when it's done.

Over the past year, I have interviewed nearly 100 people, inside and outside the church, about what they like in an online experience. I asked them to think about the sites they love and use regularly in their lives and tell me what they like about them and why they keep going back.

It is interesting to me that all answers revolved around clarity, ease of use and authenticity. Nobody ever said anything about cool technology or awesome design. Everybody said no Web site is better than a bad one.

I found a list on tonymorganlive.com that drives this point home using church site features as examples. It is just too good to leave out.

Ten easy ways to keep me from visiting your church because I visited your Web site

1. Avoid telling me what's going to happen at your church this weekend. I found churches that had prominent information about upcoming golf scrambles, but nothing about this weekend's service. Why would I come if I don't know what I'm going to experience?

2. Put a picture of your building on the main page. After all, ministry is all about the buildings.

3. Use lots of purple and pink and add pictures of flowers. Really. Are you expecting any men to show up? And, for my benefit, please don't put any doves on your Web site. Doves scare me.

4. Make me click a "skip intro" or "enter site" link. I don't have time for that, and it's very annoying. If I have to wait for something to load or have to click around intro pages to get to the real information, I'm probably going to skip your church service.

5. Add as many pictures and graphics as you can to the main page. My life is already complicated. I don't have time to figure out what's important at your church. If you dump everything on the main page, I'm assuming you don't know what's important, either.

6. Use amateur photography. And, for the record, it would be helpful to have at least one normal looking person on your site.

7. List every single ministry you have at your church. Frankly, I don't care what ministries you have. I just want to know whether or not I should visit your church this weekend. My first step isn't the men's Bible study or joining your church's prayer partner's ministry.

8. Make it as difficult as possible for me to get directions, services times, or find information about what will happen with my kids. It's important that my kids have a great experience. If you can't convince me that that will happen, I'm probably not going to risk visiting your service.

9. Put a picture of your pastor with his wife on the main page. That tells me it's all about a personality, and I see enough of those people on television. I actually found one church that had not one but two pictures of the senior pastor on the main page.

10. Try to sell your church rather than telling me how I will benefit from the experience. I don't care how great your church is. I just want to know if visiting your church will help me and my friends take our next steps toward Christ.[3]

Technology and design can enhance or hinder the experience, but they don't make it.

HOW TO DRIVE PEOPLE TO THE WEB

I will say this up front: if your audience does not depend on the Internet for life outside your church, these next few pages might not be for you. But, if your audience is paying bills online, watching YouTube, blogging, checking email daily, etc., you might be trying to figure out how to move people to the Web for information. Some thoughts about how to make the move:

- **Reduce the amount of information you print.** If you make the information available in multiple spots, people won't get used to going to one place to find it. Only make it available on the Web; people get used to looking for it on the Web.

- **Use the paper content to drive people to the Web.** For example, replace your brochure with a 4 x 6 postcard that will drive people online to register, print maps, etc. They get prompting on paper and get the rest of the story online.

- **Don't create handouts for your info counter.** Instead, put a computer at the counter, and train your guest services team to use the Web site for their source of information. Make it easy for them; condense things on two to four main landing pages so they can quickly find the answers to commonly asked questions (e.g., events, volunteer opportunities, weekend series, etc.).

- **Design it once; use it twice.** If your audience is split (half online and half off), you can serve both audiences without duplicating efforts. Create the content and promotions online with the intent of printing the page on-demand at guest services for people who don't go online.

- **Give online users the scoop on content.** Share the weekend series trailer before it's shown in the service. Reveal details not available in the bulletin. Create downloadable resources that extend the weekend service (e.g., discussion guides, Bible readings, etc.). Create a value for going online, not an online version of what is already available in print.

- **Drive people to the hub.** Print the web address everywhere—service slides, the bulletin, every handout, etc. Make it easy and clear that the one-stop place to visit for all information is this one Web site. The more web addresses you drive people to, the more confusing it is. Don't make it hard for people to try to figure out where to go for what and to remember which is which. It is more effective and unifying to promote one URL that links to other pages or sites.

- **Eliminate redundancy.** If you have multiple sites for various ministries and departments, make sure they link back to the main site for content that affects 80% of the audience. Content that is replicated across multiple sites creates extra work for you and increases the margin for error.

- **Make your site navigation simple.** A Web site with ten basic HTML pages can be more helpful, trustworthy and effective than a high-powered Web site with one hundred pages. More menu choices do not equal more value.

CURB YOUR ENTHUSIASM

There are some common misperceptions about what makes a great Web site:

- The best way to win is to copy the competition.

- Our Web site should explain everything about us.

- It should be slick with lots of bells and whistles.

Do you want to know what to include on your Web site? It starts by knowing what not to include. Self-control is the only way to go.

- **Don't reinvent the wheel.** Trying to be all things to all people doesn't work. What is the most important thing? Make that your priority. Why do you need a weather bug on the church Web site? People aren't counting on the church for their weather report or local news.

- **It's ok to leave them wanting more.** Your Web site *supports* your communications; it is not the *communicator*. You don't need to tell them everything. Help them find what's happening next and how to be a part of it. Help pull them into the action, instead of assuming they prefer to sit passively on the sidelines reading pages of copy.

- **Web users are task-driven.** High-tech gimmicks may look great but they load slowly. You have about three seconds to hook them. It's better to leave it out rather than make people wait.

- **Count the cost.** If you can't maintain it, don't implement it. An outdated site is an outdated church.

- **It's not Times Square.** Don't overpower people because you can. Use small icons and shorter event descriptions to highlight what matters instead of forcing people to weed through an endless barrage of stuff that doesn't.

- **Don't put the IT or graphics guru in charge.** The designated driver of your web vehicle doesn't function as a web master but as a user-advocate, balancing the needs of the organization between the needs of the audience. They manage the project and set priorities through an all-church filter. Graphics and IT decisions should be supporting players, not the lead character.

It takes a lot of self-control to limit your online content, but you should be the one working hard at it so the people on your site don't have to.

THINK IT OVER

Adopting the best practice—untangle the Web.

☐   If my Web site is an environment where people gather and might bring their friends, what am I doing to make it inviting? Why would people want to come back after they visit it once?

☐   What percentage of my resources (time and money) am I allocating for maintenance? For upgrades? Which has the bigger impact?

☐   What changes can I make to become a web servant instead of a web master?

☐   Can I list some of my favorite Web sites (not church Web sites) and determine what I like about them and what keeps me coming back? What's the connection?

☐   How hard are we making people work on our site? Is information easy to find? Or, is it easy to get lost?

part 3

THE RESPONSIBILITY OF GETTING BUY-IN

What starts with the best intentions for leading change often turns to defeat or defensiveness. The candid truth? Most of us are ineffective because we are pushing our own agenda—our way. What we think is the right way. Under pressure to demonstrate results quickly, we have the tendency to skip crucial "soft skills"—the emotional intelligence quotient—of our job. Even with an increased awareness of a better communication strategy, few understand how to get buy-in and manage it. Ric Willmot, a professional executive consultant, paints a great picture of what's at risk when we underestimate the importance of the "people" side of our job: "Without buy-in, strategy remains on the tarmac and the flight remains at the end of the runway."[1]

chapter 11

REWRITE YOUR
JOB DESCRIPTION

Even though you might have all the talent, technique, tools and tricks on your side regarding graphics, creativity, copywriting, etc., you won't get very far if the people you work with think you're an idiot or a controlling bully. I'm not saying you ARE these things, but people might *think* you are. Do you ever notice your best intentions are met with lackluster reactions from those around you? Not only *can* you do something about it, you *should* do something about it. That's the part of this job that is too often ignored.

MY BOSS DOESN'T GET IT

I've noticed a primary theme over the past few years as I've interacted with people asking how to lead change in their organizational communications strategy (or lack of strategy). People are often frustrated and defeated in their jobs trying to get staff to "follow the rules."

There, my friends, is the root of the problem. The challenge typically isn't with a pastor or boss who "doesn't get it" or with an uncooperative staff, but with the person who is trying to get "staff to mind" in the first place.

Many times our M.O.* is the culprit; we take ourselves too seriously trying to get the job done our way. We don't consciously realize this is often our driving force, but underneath it all, it's there. If we purify and change our objective, we will see a dramatic change in the results—not just for the people who attend our church, but also for the people with whom we work and serve.

Instead of asking questions such as, "How do I convince my boss that we need to run everything through me before we print it?" or "How do I get people to follow the logo guidelines?", the questions should be "How can I clear hurdles to help people do their best work?" and "Am I doing what I need to do so others can do what they need to do?"

Elbert Hubbard said,

> **"If men could only know each other, they would neither idolize nor hate."**[1]

Pause for a minute to let that sink in. That quote should have a significant impact. Its point is key to leading change in an organization.

---

* Mode of operation.

People are attached to comfort zones, and change typically involves driving people from their comfort zones (even when the change is good). If we're not sensitive to that reality, it has negative consequences on teamwork and flow.

If you want your leaders and staff peers to care about what you do, you need first to show your staff and leaders how much you care about what they do.

- If you are always in the office at 7 a.m., switch up your schedule to see who is hanging around the office late at night.

- If you are a late owl, attend a couple of early morning meetings to see what people do in the daylight.

- Show up at a student gathering just to observe the unique opportunities and challenges for leaders in that environment.

- Attend an event you wouldn't normally attend, just to show support to your peers.

That always means the change is going to take longer than you want it to, but the alternative is failure to launch.

MORE THAN ONE AUDIENCE

I brought a lot of practical and technical experience from the corporate world when I joined the staff team at Granger. But, even with everything I had going for me, it took about two years before I really started making an impact. I was spinning my wheels until I learned some valuable life lessons, and those lessons came to me in a place I didn't expect—my own family.

Ironically enough, I (Little Miss Communications Director) had gone on autopilot and had stopped learning about one of the audiences in my own home—my teenage daughter, Erin. She acted out and dramatic events played out to get my attention. It got ugly and embarrassing during a very tumultuous and eye-opening season. Relationships were strained, and the only way to get through it was to call a time-out.

I changed my schedule, cut the fluff and intentionally focused more on Erin. I flip-flopped my approach from talking and teaching (all about me) to watching and learning (all about her). I was able to appreciate and understand her perspective in a whole new light, and it completely changed how I communicate with her. Our relationship improved tenfold.

The lessons I learned at home opened my eyes to why my efforts in the office weren't yielding positive results. Aha. I had been spending all of my time thinking about *my* message instead of thinking about the people (my co-workers) on the other side of the message. The communications principles I preach about so passionately? Turns out, they apply to external *and* internal audiences—in the office *and* in the home. Am I the only one who didn't get that?

DESCRIBE WHAT YOU DO

The generic job description for a communications director varies widely, depending on the environment. I've seen it all on the continuum from receptionist to graphic artist to media agent to fundraiser. The first time somebody asked me about my job description, I answered in two words—**consumer advocate.**

So, what are the job responsibilities of a consumer advocate?

- Embrace the mission, vision and values of the organization. Live it and love it.

- Protect the audience from bad experiences in both print and media touchpoints.

- Work on behalf of the audience to uncover their needs, and make it easy for them to find next steps to meet them.

- Identify barriers and distractions and remove them.

- Develop relationships across the organization's stakeholders to develop strategies and tactics for new approaches.

- Develop processes that help cut through the clutter.

- Help people connect with resources and each other without going through a middleman.

- Eliminate information overload.

And, the qualifications for a consumer advocate?

- In touch with audience and management simultaneously and the ability to convey different visions to both.

- Enthusiasm for the job is obvious and contagious.

- Access to a network of relevant professionals—writers, designers, creative directors, developers, production managers, etc.

That's a great start. But what if I only have an elevator ride to explain the job description and qualifications? I would summarize them like this:

> Your church has a message. A message of truth, hope and purpose. But, before people in your congregation or community encounter that message, they encounter your church. Your job, as communications director, is to maximize the things in your church that attract people to the message and remove the things that repel them. The ultimate objective? To deliver a cohesive, unified experience at every place someone comes in contact with your church—the touchpoints.

You might be wearing more than one hat, and there's something I don't want you to miss. **Whether you are the receptionist, the senior pastor's assistant, an associate pastor or any other role in your organization, you can take on the role of communications director without any title to support it.** It's not the title that makes any difference; it's the perspective you have in your existing role that makes the difference. What's stopping you from being a consumer advocate?

COMFORT THE DISTURBED—
DISTURB THE COMFORTABLE

I read this one-liner on a t-shirt while I was on vacation. "Comfort the disturbed. Disturb the comfortable." Immediately, I thought, "YES!" Not only is this what we should *be doing*, it's what we *need*. I adopted it as my secondary mantra.*

We—human beings, Christians and churches—have the tendency to present things from our side of the table—our perspective only. We'll seek out resources that support our viewpoint and avoid things that don't.

It's uncomfortable and messy when we expose ourselves to perspectives that swing outside our lines. And, people don't like being uncomfortable. Especially people in church. **If we're too comfortable, we need to be disturbed.**

When we're too comfortable, we're smug and quick to judge. This is why the rest of the line is so important. My pastor, Mark Beeson, said it this way, "Don't live out your faith by calling the police on people when they need an ambulance." **If people are disturbed, we need to comfort them.**

I'm as guilty as the next guy, and it takes work in my personal life not to live in my own "bubble." One way I try to learn about what's disturbing others is to read books that fall outside the lines I've drawn for myself. Last year, I read a few that I probably wouldn't leave out on my desk; one was counter to my core belief system, and the others were explicitly vulgar at times. One of the books I read was about a subject I have absolutely zero interest in, but I read it anyway because it's of interest to someone I work with.**

---

* If you don't know my first mantra by now, you're just not paying attention. Less clutter, less noise!

** Because sometimes, the person that needs the most comforting is the one sitting at the desk right next to us.

I can't say these books will necessarily show up on my recommended reading list, but I can say I learned from every one of them, and that not a single one of them was a waste of my time. Each book revealed a condition of human nature or culture to which I was blind.

"Comfort the disturbed. Disturb the comfortable." Let it sink in. Then, figure out what you're going to do about it.

YOU DON'T NEED A TITLE TO BE A LEADER

It bums me out when I hear people say, "I can't do anything about it because I'm not in charge." Lack of power in an organization doesn't always equate to lack of influence. Have you ever heard of "leading up"? It is how to get things done and motivate others without formal authority.

Mark Sanborn wrote a book about it, *You Don't Need a Title to Be a Leader*. In it, he listed a few ingredients to leading without the virtue of power or position.

- **Self-mastery.** Develop your competence, character and connection. Focused attention on your sphere of influence beats brains, brawn and technology every time.

- **Power *with* people rather than power *over* people.** Don't strive to be likeable or capable, but a balance of both.

- **Implementation Quotient.** This is the ability to execute. Don't just talk about what needs to be done; take ownership, and make it happen.

- **Persuasive Communication Skills.** Influence others; don't force-feed your agenda.

- **Giving.** Giving of everything—yourself, your time, your knowledge.

According to the latest research, IQ accounts for only 4% to 10% of career success.[2] More important are the "soft aptitudes"—the qualities tougher to quantify such as imagination, joyfulness and social dexterity. You may know your stuff, but until you expand your toolbox and master these qualities, you're not going to stand out.

WHAT DO YOU DO WHEN YOU ARE BUZZED?

Everybody talks about how to create buzz.* But, nobody talks about what to do when you actually get it.

In February 2006, our church ran a five-week message series where you could find straight talk and answers about sex. It was not what people were expecting from a church. And, that was precisely the point.

To help promote the series, we used billboard advertising around town that featured one photo (bare feet entwined under bed covers) and one line of text—mylamesexlife.com. Curious onlookers who visited mylamesexlife.com saw a brief movie asking questions that commonly surround the topic of sex. At the end of the movie, viewers were redirected to GCCwired.com to learn more about the upcoming weekend series called PureSex.

It sparked controversy and conversations around our community and got national attention. The response—positive and negative—was overwhelming. It created a stir. But, I'm not going to talk about the advertising we did or the media attention that resulted from the series.** I'm going to answer the question nobody's asking (but should). What did we do with the buzz once we got it?

That's the hidden landmine in creating buzz. Everyone is so busy trying to manufacture buzz, but few are prepared for it when it comes.

What happens when you get what you were hoping for? What happens when the crowds come in droves? Or, the phone is ringing off the hook? Or, every media outlet is wanting a sound

* Buzz is the excitement, energy, anticipation and conversation around a product or service. It's the best type of marketing—when "people are buzzing."
** mylamesexlife.com has all the details if you're looking for the rest of the story.

bite? Things can go sideways before you realize it, and then you start feeding the frenzy around you. In the process, you can lose sight of what you came to do in the first place. It's dangerous for anyone, *especially* if you are in the church.

We didn't set out to create a flurry of activity, but to create a helpful series about sex for people who weren't hearing the truth from anyone, anywhere about the subject of sex. We tried a few things that people don't expect from a church, hoping people would be curious enough at least to come check it out. And, that is what created a flurry of activity.*

I'll admit, it even threw *me* off when we started getting calls from the national media. My mind automatically short-circuited into figuring out ways to manipulate a new message with an expanded platform positively. It's easy to freeze like a deer in headlights when you are in the spotlight, but it's just as easy to avoid being surprised if you've prepared for it and stick to your original goal. If you can't say what that goal is, then you're not ready.

When I asked my senior pastor if he was nervous about the television anchors on their way over with a camera crew, here is how he responded. He remembered the original goal.

> This is not new for us; it's what we do all day, every day. People matter to God, and we're just loving people one at a time. I'm not nervous. Reporters are people, too. They matter to God, and they matter to us. It's just another day at Granger Community Church.

Even with a flurry of buzz—local, regional, national—communication isn't complicated. The old rule still applies—less is more. Were we expecting Fox News in New York or Mancow in

---

* But, really, between you and me, we didn't come up with anything that shakes the core of culture. I still can't believe it got the media attention it did. A church teaches what the Bible says about sex and advertises the series with bare feet on a billboard. Is it really that newsworthy? I still don't get that part of it. Anyway, back to the story.

Chicago to call us about the series? No. But, when they did, our senior pastor was prepared. You see, he knew the message never changed. It wasn't about the billboards, the Web site, the media or the sex. He started and stayed with the same message from beginning to end—"People matter to God." Plain and simple.

THINK IT OVER

The responsibility of buy-in—rewrite your job description.

☐ What am I doing to show my co-workers I care about what they do?

☐ How do my actions portray a different me from the one I want people to see? What "soft aptitudes" do I need to develop?

☐ Do I recognize the multiple audiences I serve? Or, am I focusing on one at the expense of all the others? Am I living by the same rules with my co-workers as I do with church guests and members?

☐ What am I doing to get uncomfortable to learn about the people who need my comfort?

☐ How can I put my own best interests aside to foster a collaborative environment? What gifts can I give others, even if the "gift" is humor, understanding or knowledge. What else can I give?

☐ Am I asking questions such as, "How do I convince my boss that we need to…" or "How do I get people to follow the guidelines?" when I should be asking "How can I clear hurdles to help my boss do his job?" and "Am I doing what I need to do so others can do what they need to do?"

☐ How can I describe what I do? What am I an advocate for? What change will I make if I am successful?

chapter 12
ASK, DON'T TELL

Effective communication depends on a common vocabulary. Do you know the vocabulary from other departments in your organization or just yours? Knowing how to carry on a dialogue is more important than forcefully proclaiming what you know. The people in charge are supposed to have all the answers, right? I am going to assume you are smart enough to know the answer to that question is no. One size does not fit all. The most effective team-builders make time to hear from others about their unique audience needs, department hurdles, system problems and team pain points. You will gain insight and credibility by leading your conversations and running your projects—big or small—with more questions than directives.

GET AN IMAGE CONSULTANT

I read somewhere that the top three reasons people don't want to work with the corporate communications (or marketing) department are:

1. They're controlling.

2. They don't have a clue as to what I do in my job.

3. They make things harder and get in the way.

Do you know how you come across to others? What are people saying about you when you are not around? Do they think you are controlling, clueless and make things harder? Don't feel bad. Sometimes, it comes with the territory.

But, there is good news in all of this. Perception is reality for some people. And, when you are aware of what that perception is, you can do something about it.

I wanted to know what people were saying about our team, so I had a friend set up a camera at our staff meeting and ask people to answer the question, "What was your first impression of the communications department?" We gave people permission to be candid and assured them the feedback would be helpful. It was an intentional step to demonstrate we care more about how our actions make people feel than how to get them to do what we want.

That exercise proved to be more valuable than I anticipated. I was able to draw upon the wisdom of others with diverse perspectives.

When I heard from people who think differently than me, my blind spots were revealed to me. Here are some of the things that were said.

- "Why do we need them?"

- "Trouble."

- "A force to be worked around, overcome and ignored."

Right then and there, I decided I needed to figure out a way to get helpful feedback like this on an ongoing basis.

For the past two years, I have leaned on two trustworthy image consultants at the office: Tim Stevens (my friend and boss) and Jami Ruth (my friend and co-worker). These people really know me and my tendencies. I process with them before I act—testing my theories, previewing my plans, sharing my frustrations and pitching my solutions. **They help me anticipate problems, offer advocacy when needed and put professional guardrails in place to save me from *me*.**

Everybody should find at least two image consultants in the workplace: one who helps process *your effect on individuals* and another who helps process *your effect on the crowd*. It's good to have a boss and a peer on your image team—two honest people who are on your side with a front row seat to your strengths and weaknesses. They'll save you from *you*.

LEADING THE WITNESS

A friend of mine had the title of Communications Director but said it should be changed to Communications Redirector because he spent 50% of his time redirecting people and projects. I think it is a fair perspective and good example to follow, regardless of what your role or job title may be.

But, there is tension in that, isn't there? Sometimes there is tension because people are coming to you to get something done. They really aren't interested in being "re-directed" or processing more questions with you. Other times, the tension is there because what they're asking you for isn't going to help them. In fact, it might even hinder them—and you know it. But, they didn't come for you to tell them they're wrong. You can't sell what they're not looking for.

Every conversation and project has different dynamics, but if you can find a system that helps you avoid spending too much time creating or too much time regulating, it's a win. It's never a win if you consistently find yourself playing the role of the communications police. One way is to start every project with a healthy skepticism and simply… ask questions.

Somebody smart told me about the three areas they evaluate for everything they do. I don't remember the *who**, but the *what* stuck, and it is a system we use. Here are the three areas we use as a filter to evaluate everything we do and some of the questions we ask along the way.

- **Is it appealing (context)?** Are we focusing our energy from the "inside out" or from the "outside in"? Do we know why people will spend their time and attention on us? Does it apply to their life in a practical way? What makes it worth the hassle? Do we know the comfort zone?

* Whoever you are, I'm sorry I forgot about you.

- **Is it engaging (presentation)?** Are we unifying our message or diluting it? Are we reducing the noise in people's life or adding to it? Are we removing the barriers to entry? What problem is this solving? Does this support or compete with the intended experience for our audience? Are we making things easy for them to find? Easy to understand? Easy to do?

- **Is it helpful (content)?** Are we giving people what they want, when they want it? Or, are we answering questions they haven't asked yet? What expectations are we setting that are unrealistic or out of our control? Are we promising something we can't deliver on? Are we making statements as if they were facts, when in reality they are subjective and left to personal interpretation? Are we baiting people with exaggerated benefits?

Sometimes, you are leading the witness with your questioning; other times, the two-way collaboration comes naturally. Either way, the result is breakthrough thinking and new insights from everyone on the same page.

TEST ASSUMPTIONS

I read something in a magazine article that reminded me how completely unnatural it is for us to actually get out of our own way.

The human eye has a blind spot in its field of vision. The human mind has something similar. Sometimes you can't "see" new information because you are bound by filters and lack the mental framework to make sense of what your eyes take in. People often see what they want to see and ignore information that doesn't fit their preconceptions. We default to the shortcut of seeing things the same way. People seek stability and security, so seeing things in a way that confirms their beliefs gives them both.[1]

We revert to autopilot, and it takes intentionality and practice to disable that habit of:

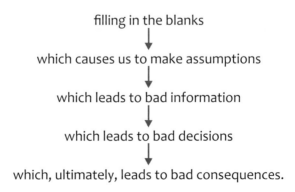

filling in the blanks
↓
which causes us to make assumptions
↓
which leads to bad information
↓
which leads to bad decisions
↓
which, ultimately, leads to bad consequences.

Those consequences could be a missed opportunity, a damaged relationship, an ineffective outreach, a dying church, a broken life or a fractured community.

Did you hear about the time the Mount St. Helen's live web cam was blocked...by a fly?

Mount St. Helens - 11 September 2005 - 12:11:00 Pacific Daylight Time

Johnston Ridge Observatory - Mount St. Helens National Volcanic Monument

What an image![2]

The big picture (a massive volcano) is lost because of the speck (an itty-bitty insect) on the lens. This happens personally and corporately. The closer we are to the "fly," the harder it is for us to see around it. We lose effectiveness in our perspective, our judgment and our communication when we lose sight of the big picture.

It is our responsibility to acknowledge that nine times out of ten, there is more to the story. Before we leap to conclusions—about a person, a method, a decision, a program—we should learn about it. When we are deliberate about doing our homework, it is amazing the new wisdom, impact and connection that opens up to us.

Untested assumptions, preconceived notions, wrong conclusions—they all impair your sight.

Is there a fly in your environment that is blocking your view? Marcia Connor said, "Help yourself see more by looking past your beliefs." What have we fallen in love with that is not as effective as it used to be? Where are we working hard with little return? What are we doing out of habit without remembering why? Where are we manufacturing energy? Why does my mom cut the ends off her pot roast?*

Test your assumptions, dig in with some questions and clean your lens.

---

* If you don't get this reference, this story might be helpful. You can find a variety of versions on the Internet, but here's the gist. A mother was preparing pot roast for Sunday's big family dinner. Before placing it in the pan, she carefully sliced the ends off. Her five-year-old daughter asked, "Mommy, why do you cut the ends off?" She answered, "My mom taught me to do it that way, and it's delicious, so it must be a good idea." When everyone sits down for dinner, the daughter remembers the question and asks, "Grandma, why did you teach Mommy to cut the ends off the roast?" Grandma smiled and said, "It's the only way I could get it to fit in my small pan."

MY TEAM DISAGREES WITH ME

I believe the best team members are the ones who communicate what they think. There is no penalty for disagreement. And, for the record, people on my team frequently disagree with me. I am frequently wrong.

But, I don't take that personally. And, neither do they.

I believe in (and thrive in) a culture that promotes honesty with each other about everything. Not honesty in the context of negativity, irrelevant advice or directionless opinions, but honesty in an environment that allows people to express what they see, even if that means they see something different from what I see.

No. Make that, *especially* when they see something different from what I see.

Because, when my team members feel free to be honest about what they see, it allows me to see the entire picture—the sum of opinions—to make decisions about what needs to be done. Just last week, I asked one of my team members to complete a project. Twenty-four hours later, that team member came back to me and said, "I don't think we should do this. I don't think it will be helpful, and here's why." After I had the chance to ask a few questions, it turns out—they were right.

This only works when the team starts with a unified vision. Because, let's face it—every dysfunctional team out there disagrees all the time. That makes it hard for team members to agree at the end of the day on what needs to be done for the success of the team because the "success of the team" has never been defined. There is no shared agreement that "we are all pulling in the same direction." People only focus on their own part or opinion.

Once you have that unified vision of the big picture, keep the unity by leaving room to disagree about how to get there. This type of culture allows everyone to wrestle with each other over an idea, to see all sides and land on our feet to move forward better, faster and stronger* together than they ever could alone.

You know who else likes a team not afraid to disagree with him? Ed Catmull, co-founder and president of Pixar Animation Studios.** The *Harvard Business Review* wrote an entire article about how he manages creative people to foster a collaborative environment. His secret to success isn't telling people what to do; it's inviting opinions from the people around him. And, it seems to be working. He has a pretty productive gig.

Wouldn't you agree? It is ok if you don't. I won't take it personally.

---

* Shout out to Proverbs 27:17! *Just like iron sharpens iron; friends sharpen the minds of each other.*
** You know, the makers of *Monsters, Inc.*, *The Incredibles*, *Finding Nemo*, *Toy Story*, etc.

TREAT PEOPLE AS IF THEY'RE SMART

The need for control is a challenge that nearly all of us wrestle with. That impulse kicks in and before we realize it, we tell people how they should think. Just ask my husband if I can ride silently in the passenger seat.* We all have fallen victim to the tendency, and every time we allow the impulse to take over, it magnifies stress and works against us, especially in the workplace.

Nobody likes to be controlled. **They like it when you get them thinking, but not when you tell them what to think.**

I found a quote by Guy Kawasaki, author and entrepreneur, that should get you thinking.**

———————————————— ●●●●● ————————————————

I believe that people are inherently smart. If you provide them with the right information, they are the best judges of the suitability of your product or service. I don't believe you should—or can—bludgeon people into becoming a customer. My recommendation is that you enable people to test drive your product or service in order to make their own decision. Essentially, you are saying, "I think you're smart. Because I think you're smart, I'm going to enable you to try my product to see if it works for you. I hope that it does and that we can do business."[3]

———————————————— ●●●● ————————————————

How does this affect your agenda? In essence, you are selling yourself and your ideas as a service product, right? Remember, products and services are "bought," not sold. You can't sell what people aren't asking for. So, are your co-workers saying, "Thank

---

* I asked him for you. He said, "sometimes," which is a major improvement. A few years ago, his answer would have been "never."
** Jason Powell, our IT Director, found it first. He shares smart stuff at jpowell.blogs.com.

you!" instead of "Why do we have to do this?" The difference between treating people as if they're smart and as if they don't have a brain is the difference between placing blame and sharing, forcing and encouraging.

What a novel idea: treat people as if they're smart, and ask them what they think. They will champion what works and reveal what doesn't.

THINK IT OVER

The responsibility of buy-in—ask; don't tell.

☐   Do I know how I come across to others? Are there times when my message comes across cold and harsh when that is not my intent? Do I act as if I have all the answers, or do I leave room for non-consensus?

☐   Am I afraid to hear full perspective from others, or are others afraid to share it with me because of my argumentative reaction?

☐   People are better art critics than they are artists. How can I give them the ability to comment without having to make them create?

☐   Am I so close to the mechanics that I've lost sight of the big picture? What speck on my lens is getting in the way of the big picture? What fly do we have in our organizational environment blocking the view of the mountain? Do we have fly swatters on our team?

☐   What opportunities do I have to redirect communications—in my department or for my organization? Do I have a healthy skepticism toward every project until we're able to process the context, presentation and content? Do I evaluate things to make sure they are appealing, engaging and helpful? Or, do I just create things without running them through any filter?

chapter 13

FIND THE YES BEHIND THE NO

When you are asked to think differently or change the way you have always done something, does it tend to evoke some type of emotion? Especially when we are already under pressure, it's hard not to react to unexpected directives with anger, defensiveness, alienation or frustration. What do you think happens when we come at others with some new policy, system or restriction? Yep. Like you, they have a hard time not taking it personally. So, try a different approach. When you do find it necessary to introduce a new process or guideline, find ways to implement it as a helpful framework with room to move, not a rigid policy. Instead of coming at people, come alongside them.

FREEDOM WITHIN A FRAMEWORK

One of the guiding principles on my team is "Freedom within a Framework." The "freedom" means we don't boss people around with a list of rules. The "framework" is the guidelines we give them to work within. Our job is about harnessing the power of a message and enhancing the experience, not about the do's and don'ts. There is a balance between centralizing efforts that maximize excellence and creating a bottleneck for the things that don't matter. Do you know how to evaluate that contrast?

Let's use me as an example. A few years ago, as more and more of our staff started personal blogs, I was asked to write some guidelines for our staff handbook. Here was my first draft; it was several pages long.* Feel free to scan it.

Granger Blogging Policies

Some Granger Community Church employees who maintain personal Web sites and/ or blogs, or who are considering beginning one, have asked about the church's perspective regarding these sites. In general, we view personal Web sites and blogs positively, and respect the right of our employees to use them as an avenue of self-expression and outreach.

As an employee of Granger Community Church, you are seen by our members and outside parties as a representative of the church. Therefore, as in all areas of daily life, a church staff member's personal Web site or blog is a reflection on the church, whether or not the church is specifically discussed or referenced. If you choose to identify yourself as a Granger Community Church employee or to discuss matters related to the church on your Web site or blog, please bear in mind that, although you may view your site as a personal project, many readers will assume you are speaking on behalf of the church.

In light of this possibility, Granger expects our staff to observe the following important guidelines:

* You might enjoy knowing that the finished product is an inspired hybrid from the blogging policies of IBM, Yahoo, Sun and Fellowship Church. They did all of the heavy lifting for us.

Notify Your Supervisor. If you currently have a personal Web site or blog, or are considering starting one, be sure to discuss this with your supervisor.

Include a Disclaimer. On your site, please make it clear to your readers that the views you express are yours alone and that they do not necessarily reflect the views of Granger Community Church. To help reduce the potential for confusion, we recommend you prominently display the following notice, or something similar, on the home page of your site:

> *I work at Granger Community Church. Everything here, however, is my personal opinion and is not read or approved before it is posted. Opinions, conclusions and other information expressed here do not necessarily reflect the views of Granger Community Church.*

We recommend a disclaimer if your site is published under your name, even if it is entirely personal and does not mention Granger Community Church or your employment, as readers will inevitably connect your personal life to your professional life.

Respect Confidentiality. You must take proper care not to purposefully or inadvertently disclose any information that is confidential or proprietary to Granger Community Church. Be sure that what you are announcing has been in the weekend bulletin, on the Web site, or announced from the stage before posting it. Otherwise, check with your supervisor. Any employee who violates our policies regarding confidentiality will be subject to serious discipline, up to and including immediate termination of employment.

Respect the Church and Its Staff. Since your site is a public space, we expect you to be respectful to the church and our leaders, employees, volunteers and members. Any employee who uses a personal Web site to disparage the name or reputation of the church, its practices, or its pastors, officers, employees, volunteers or members will be subject to serious discipline, up to and including immediate termination of employment.

Respect your Audience. Don't use ethnic slurs, personal insults, obscenity, etc., and show proper consideration for others' privacy and for topics that may be considered objectionable or inflammatory. Don't pick fights, be the first to correct your own mistakes. Try to add value. Provide worthwhile information and perspective.

Respect Your Time. All time and effort spent on your personal site should be done on your personal time and should not interfere with your job duties or work commitments.

Respect Our Beliefs. When working for a church, it is important to remember that employment decisions will be made based upon our Christian beliefs. If your personal Web site displays inappropriate images or reflects personal opinions or lifestyle choices that are contrary to Granger Community Church's beliefs, you may be subject to discipline, up to and including immediate termination of employment. For this reason, we encourage you first to seek guidance from your supervisor if you have any questions.

Respect Copyright. You may provide a link from your site to GCCwired.com or WiredChurches.com, if you wish. Contact a member of the communications group for graphics. Please do not use other church trademarks or logos on your site or reproduce material without first obtaining permission.

Follow the Staff Handbook. Consult your staff handbook and staff statement of ethics for guidance. As with other forms of communication, do not engage in personal, racial or sexual harassment, unfounded accusations or remarks that would contribute to a hostile workplace.

Use Common Sense. Use common sense in all communications, particularly on a mass communication vehicle like a Web site that is accessible to anyone. What you say on your site could potentially be grounds for dismissal. If you would not be comfortable with your manager, co-workers or the executive team reading your words, do not write them.

If you have any questions about these guidelines or any matter related to your site that these guidelines do not address, please direct them to your supervisor or the communications department, as appropriate.

For the record, this is a *bad* example of freedom within a framework. It went overboard with all of the "discipline" and "immediate termination" references. Not to mention, it goes into exhaustive detail with a condescending tone that doesn't really foster a workplace that says, "I think you're smart and believe in you." It's a good thing I ran this first draft by my image consultants*. They sent me back to the drawing board.

Here is the final draft. One page.

---

* Remember, we talked about this in Chapter 12? Get an image consultant. No, seriously. Do it.

Personal Blog Best Practices

We've developed this document to help equip staff team members who maintain personal blogs and/or post on other people's blogs. These recommendations provide a roadmap for constructive, respectful and productive dialogue between bloggers and their audience (whoever that may be). These are not "rules" and can't be broken. There is no hidden meaning or agenda. We consider these to be "best practices guidelines" that are in the spirit of our culture and the best interest of the church, whether you blog or not. We encourage you to follow these guidelines, but it is not mandatory to do so. It's your choice. We really mean that.

Be Respectful. Be thoughtful and accurate in your posts, respectful of how others may be affected. Even if your site is published under your name, is entirely personal and does not mention Granger Community Church or your employment, readers will inevitably connect your personal life to your professional life. It's a good idea to include a disclaimer on your home page that states your opinions are personal. And, just to avoid any surprises, think about giving your manager a courtesy head's up about your blog's existence.

Engage in Private Feedback. Not everyone who is reading your blog will feel comfortable approaching you if they are concerned their feedback will become public. In order to maintain an open dialogue everyone can comfortably engage in, welcome "off-blog" feedback from colleagues who would like to respond privately, make suggestions, or report errors without having their comments appear on your blog. Bloggers want to know what you think. If you have an opinion, correction or criticism regarding a blog post, reach out for the blogger directly. Whether privately or on their blog, let the blogger know your thoughts.

Legal Stuff. When you choose to go public with your opinions on your blog, you are legally responsible for your commentary. Individual bloggers can be held personally liable for any commentary deemed to be defamatory, obscene (not swear words, but rather the legal definition of "obscene"), proprietary or libelous. In essence, you blog (or comment on other people's blogs) at your own risk. Outside parties actually can pursue legal action against you for postings. It's probably not a high risk in our line of work, but we thought you'd like to know.

Use Common Sense. Take care not to disclose any confidential or proprietary information.

Press Inquiries. Blog postings may generate media coverage. If a member of the media contacts you about a church related blog posting, we've got trained back-up available to help you in the communications department.

This would be a good example of freedom within a framework. Notice the difference in tone? It communicates that we believe the best in you and want you to succeed. There's no need to censor or edit someone unless there's a problem.*

We get ourselves into trouble when we take the top-down approach and prioritize policy over people (unless safety is at risk). **A heart softened, even in the paperwork, is a two-way street.**

* When you do experience the rare and occasional problem, handle it with the individual instead of making an office-wide policy. It's more effective for everyone.

FOCUS ON YOUR SPHERE

Focus on your "sphere of influence." Like Stephen Covey wrote in *Seven Habits of Highly Effective People*, you should have passion for all that you do but spend the bulk of your energy on the things you can influence and change, instead of the things over which you have no control. There's that "control" word again.

The secret of harnessing the power of a message and unlocking maximum effectiveness in an organization is figuring out how to synchronize communication efforts without creating a bottleneck—to coordinate without control. This can be tricky when you have a message of which everybody owns a little piece and so many delivery channels at their disposal (i.e., letters, emails, text, blogging, brochures, Web sites). Governing every communication channel is impossible but synchronizing communications is very possible if you stay balanced and realistic. The yes behind the no? You can't control everything, but if you focus on what you can control—and you're good at it—you'll influence others by your example.

This "focus on your sphere of influence" principle isn't for people in charge of communications—it's for anyone who *communicates*. It applies to everyone, and practical examples always help. So let's have some fun with a practical example.

Let's say you're responsible for communicating ongoing news for the women's ministry department. It is great to get the word out but only when you keep it focused on your sphere. Don't send a letter or email blast to the entire church mailing list. Your list should only include the people your news affects. It is not enough just to narrow your list to all of the women in your church. Spend the extra time qualifying your distribution list to people who have expressed interest.

I speak from the audience perspective on this one. It's counter-productive when I get blasted with mailings and emails for every scrapbooking, dessert tea, retreat or mom's day out because I was born female. Because, when I do, I end up throwing away your mailing, tuning out your announcement and deleting your email without ever reading what it's about because I feel targeted. I don't know about you, but being in someone's crosshairs* is not a good feeling.

So, how do you get the word out to me about events that apply to women without tipping the scales? Relax, and let go. Don't tell me about everything—just the biggest, coolest stuff. I'll care about what you have to say because you're showing me you care about me by putting down the rifle. You'll gain my trust. I'll like you.

But, what about the other 1,000,000 opportunities you think I just HAVE to hear about? Don't worry. I'll learn about them from others. Invest all news in the people you have relationships with, and let them feed me the news through the relationships they have with me. They know my likes, dislikes, struggles and hurdles. They know what applies. If it doesn't, then I don't need to know about it. It's just noise.

I hope, by now, you're picking up on the truth that the responsibility of getting buy-in applies to external audiences (i.e., women's retreat promotions) as much as the internal ones (i.e., all-staff email).** And, the principle of focusing on your sphere of influence applies as much to the internal audience as the external ones. These habits are interchangeable and necessary with anyone you are trying to communicate with.

* Think "scope of a rifle."
** Your external audience is the public, guests and church members—your mass audience. Your internal audience includes your boss, peers, volunteers—the team you work with. The best practices and principles throughout this book apply to both. You have to be conscious of your overloaded audience on both sides and remember people are people.

WHAT DO I GET OUT OF IT?

A centralized system can free up resources across an organization by routing information and functions through a main hub. Whether it's for communications, data entry, technical support, ticket-tracking or something else, the benefits of a centralized system are:

- Increased accuracy; bad content leads to poor service

- Better accessibility; easy-to-find resources and easy-to-run reports

- A seamless flow; no conflicts or dead ends, start-to-finish distribution

- Continuity; a consistent experience across multiple touchpoints

- Reduced costs; automated manual processes and no duplicate efforts

All of this should be a good thing, right? Right. Except, many times anyone outside the central "hub" perceives the system as a bottleneck for his or her work and a loss of control over his or her job. The average person doesn't associate "systems" with "good times." And, you won't motivate anybody to replace "what they're used to" with a new policy or rule.

If you're looking for buy-in to generate momentum for a new system across your organization, you have to figure how to communicate what people "get out of it" as well as "here's what's at stake if we don't." Be conscientious about the way you say or don't say things to help express your pure intent of collaboration, not control.

Author Michael Kanazawa says it this way:

"If you believe that people hate change and that it is your job to change them, they will hate it. If you believe that people thrive on change and that your job is to unleash it, you will tap into a limitless source of ingenuity, energy and drive that will allow you to take your big ideas into big results."[1]

Say this:	Instead of this:
• Consult with you	• Create for you
• Proof	• Approve
• Weigh-in	• Authorize
• Here is what we can do	• No
• Consider this	• You should
• Hey...you've got a job to do, this will make it easier.	• Everybody has to do it this way from now on.
• We've reached a size where our old methods are hurting us instead of helping us, and here's what we need to adjust.	• Things are getting out of hand, so we're implementing a new policy.

Here's an outline to help you organize your thoughts before you roll out that new system:

- **Current reality:** Use practical examples and stories to describe the situation.

- **Solution:** Introduce one item of change and a time-line for the next couple of steps. Transitions will go so much smoother when everyone knows when and where the change is happening. Keep it simple. Allow room for questions. There is a chance you may have missed something.

- **Benefits:** Don't take anything away without giving something back. Either identify a tangible pain point that will be eliminated or a value gained because of the new system.

See how easy that is?* **"It's not that people hate change...they just hate how you're trying to change them."**[2]

---

* We've implemented quite a few new systems in our IT department this year. If you'd like to see a real-life example of this outline in action, you can find it in the "back of the book."

WHAT ABOUT THOSE STYLE GUIDES?

Mismatched communications from any organization look sloppy. Using the same logos, fonts, terms and punctuation rules give your materials a more consistent and professional look. I think a style guide* can be a good tool everyone can benefit from in the end, but it's primarily a hands-on tool for people who coordinate the bulk of your mass communications.

Here are a few things to keep in mind if you are creating a style guide:

- **Make it friendly.** Keep it less intimidating by just covering the basics and keeping it brief.

- **Use examples.** Do's and don'ts side-by-side provide a helpful contrast/comparison.

- **Give rationale.** Don't just give rules without the reasoning behind them.

- **Include at-a-glance pages.** At-a-glance pages add value with things such as a list of commonly misused or misspelled words, five things you need to know for everything we do here, where to go for help, and so on.

- **Don't re-create the wheel.** Use existing published style guides for your foundational reference book.** Your style guide is only a supplement to address the exceptions or specific elements for your environment (e.g., proper names of ministry teams).

---

* I've included a few sample pages in the back of the book from the Style Guide we created.

** We use the *Associated Press Stylebook* for English/Grammar and the *Wired Style Guide* for the Web.

- **Allow yourself room for exceptions.** Remember it is a guidebook, not a law book. On occasion, the appropriate thing to do is bend a rule rather than sacrifice a relationship. Consider the scope of the piece (how many people will it affect) to determine whether you need to issue a citation.

Now the worst thing you can do after creating a style guide is to force-feed it to your staff and volunteers as the rulebook they have to follow, or else. I'm not saying you *would* do that. But, it is a mistake made by many well-meaning people. Like, for example, me.

It was an ineffective practice I carried into Granger from the corporate marketing world. I look back and laugh. I actually distributed the style guide to every staff member (and thought he or she would love me for it). That is funny. What was I thinking?

THINK IT OVER

The responsibility of buy-in—find the yes behind the no.

- ☐ How am I helping people do what they need to do without going through me?

- ☐ Am I falling into control-freak traps such as top-down attitudes, prioritizing policies before people and dictating mandates as if I have all the answers? How can I relax and let go to give people the room to move?

- ☐ Can I identify the balance between maximizing excellence and creating a bottleneck for the things that don't matter? Do I know the difference between the two?

- ☐ What am I enforcing company-wide that may be more appropriate for a smaller group of people? What is my sphere of influence? What people should I be intentionally pouring into individually rather than trying to address corporately?

- ☐ Do I operate as if it is my job to change people or to unleash the change already inside of them?

chapter 14
BRING THE GLUE

One of the most important keys to the success of any organization is to have all parts working and pulling together, independently aligned to the same vision. This is easier said than done. Focused on their tasks, individuals have a hard time understanding how their daily decisions affect the bigger picture, how their actions have a domino effect (good and bad). Even when everyone starts in the same place, by the end of one busy day with normal demands, vision drift starts to happen. When you bring the glue, you can more easily keep people connected to the same vision, fostering collaboration and cross training that move people from spectator to participant. Find ways to create mirrors that show the parts what the whole is doing. That is the glue.

MISPLACED LOYALTIES

I purchased a Roman shade and found it damaged when I opened the package. I had the receipt. I had the original packaging. I had the product. But, the store wouldn't let me exchange it. They said that since it had been more than 90 days, they "couldn't help me." I explained that the shade was purchased for a remodeling project that was just completed. It sat unused in the box until now. All I needed was an exchange. "Sorry, that's *our policy*."

Again, I showed my receipt.

"Sorry, your receipt is expired." (Since when does money expire?)

"We don't carry that product anymore. It has no value to us." (Yes. They really said that.)

"Sorry. That's our policy." (This should be illegal. Really.)

They tried to brush me off and told me to go home and call the toll-free customer service number. I asked them to call it for me while I was standing at the desk. Surprise, surprise. After twenty minutes on the line, even they couldn't get through to a live person. Uh, huh. That's what I thought.

Here's my point. This business was more concerned and more loyal to their "policy" than they were to the customer. When I hear the *customer service* representative say "That product has no value to us anymore," it is obvious to me they could care less about customer service. Never mind the fact they sold me damaged goods. After 90 days, it's not their problem—it's mine. No matter what. Happy trails. How is that for *customer service*?

That experience, and others like it, make me wonder why more businesses don't empower their employees to champion customer satisfaction. The Roman shade was just over $60 with tax. If I were in charge, I would allow employees to make judgment calls under a certain dollar amount to retain happy customers.* I would teach them about the common sense of spreading goodwill and making a better store experience that makes people want to tell their friends and come back.

Do we keep this in mind when we deal with our teams? Do we say things such as "That's our policy," "Sorry, I can't help you," or "That's not the way we do things here"? Do we empower our staff and volunteers to use common sense and break protocol to create great experiences? **How many "do not enter" or "no drinks permitted" signs are in your lobby?** Are your greeters coached how to smile, read body language and make people feel welcome?**

I read about a great service-centric policy at Griffin Technologies.

_____ ●●● ● _____

Some companies make you jump through hoops to get a replacement for a malfunctioning device. Griffin Technology takes a rather different approach to the process by issuing replacements right away and asking only that the customer destroy the non-functioning device "in a creative manner" and send photographic evidence. One customer took the challenge to heart and decided the only sane thing to do would be to take the obvious route: blow it up with model rocket engines.[1]

_____ ● ●● ● _____

Griffin Technologies gets it. And, typically, this model works from the inside out.

* Someone told me the managers of each Enterprise Car Rental shop have the authority to quote their own rate to an individual customer even if it means a lower quote than what is advertised. That's a great example of empowering a staff to deliver customer service.
** In his book, _First Impressions_, Mark Waltz has a whole chapter of "wow-busters." I think it should be required reading for every church.

It's how superiors treat their employees and co-workers treat each other that ultimately affect how a staff treats the customer.

If you make this your mode of operation, you'll have the insight to use rules in context and develop relational collateral. If you don't, people will do everything they can to work around or ignore you. Here's how you can avoid advocating rules over people.

- **Lead with the listen.** Give leaders, peers and subordinates the space to be heard. See what you can learn from their feedback before you push the policy.

- **Drop the hall monitor badge.** It is all about relationships. Show people you are human and for the team—not for yourself.

- **Be available.** Open your door, come in the office, take off your headphones, walk around and don't hide behind email or voicemail.

- **Smoke what you're selling.** If you want other people to care about your job, show others you care about theirs. Support what they're doing—with nothing to gain, no strings attached.

Guidelines and rules are good when they bring people together. Remember who you're serving.

YOU ARE REPLACEABLE

What is the number one way to get the word out about your church (and keep people coming back)? This is for everyone—ready? Set. Go!

- Flyers? No.

- Web site? No.

- Banners? No.

- Advertising? No.

- Free stuff? No.

None of these things are bad. They all can help. But, they are supporting characters. They become ineffective when you give them the lead role in your story.

The number one way to get the word out *about* any organization is through the words and actions of the people *in* the organization. Every person in your church is like a walking billboard. How they act, work, talk, respond and treat people represents *you* and leaves a lasting impression on *others*.

It doesn't matter if your music is great. Or, if you've got fantastic design skills. Or, if your pastor is the most intelligent person on the planet. If your customer service is average or bad, your church is replaceable. Author and blogger Andy Sernowitz explains why.

Sooner or later, most customers will leave you for a company that treats them better (even if the price is a bit higher or the product is a bit worse).

I've had an eFax account for almost 10 years. It works great. But for the third year in a row, they raised the price—without telling me or even sending a receipt. I just noticed the bill on my credit card. It wasn't an issue of price. It was an issue of trying to sneak something past me. The first time was annoying, the second time I got angry. This time I walked.

I will boldly go here—before you spend money on marketing, spend money improving the people skills of your people.

Making somebody a better artist or writer isn't really what I'm talking about here. It's the human communication behavior issues such as:

- How to treat others under pressure.

- How to turn negatives into positives.

- How to redirect rather than issue a "smackdown."

- How to deal with difficult people.

- How to focus and capitalize on people's strengths rather than complain and get aggravated by their weaknesses.

Your people might need the most help with these social graces. The return on investment will blow your mind. The sustainability can't be challenged. People skills count more. And, some of your people might need help with those skills. A little shared training goes a long, long way.*

---

* Looking for a place to start? Read some books together. I've included my current top 10 must-read list in the back of the book.

TOUCHY-FEELY DATABASES

I watch organizations treat their database like a technology add-on when, in fact, it should be treated as the central lifeline for customer care. It's the digital "turnstile" for a person's connections, history, growth, safety, milestones, relationships as well as a place to find trend indicators and organizational health reports. Contrary to popular belief, the database is very "touchy-feely."

That is why we haven't assigned a technology guru or someone with mad data entry skills to be in charge of our database. We handpicked a representative from each department to form a SuperTeam.

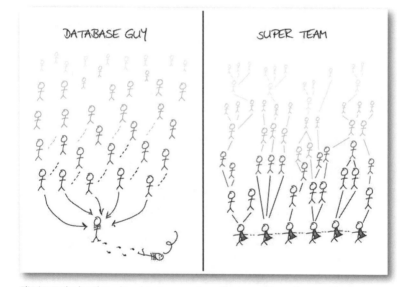

Eliminate the bottleneck and empower advocates across the entire organization.

As our organization grew, we found our organization in a place with multiple community touchpoints—each serving up a different experience, off and running in its own direction, capturing (or not capturing) their own data. When individual teams track data their own way—using systems unique to their team only—critical information gets lost or isolated. People and projects proliferate—as does confusion. This creates real liabilities for the organization as a whole. Here are just a few examples:

- People with preschoolers or who no longer had children at home consistently received letters addressed "Dear Middle School Parent."

- A family in our church lost a child. For several weeks in a row after that horrendous loss, a check-in tag for their deceased son would print at the kiosk when they checked in their other children.

- We had volunteers with serving restrictions due to moral or security reasons who would move from team to team repeating the offense because there was no central filing system to alert team leaders proactively.

- We had several people flagged as core covenant members who had not been active in the church for over six years.

- We had people who had moved out of state still flagged as attendees.

- We mailed sensitive and confidential contribution statements to the wrong address.

- A widow in our church continued to receive correspondence addressed to her deceased husband.

Not only was each event discouraging and painful for the members affected, but also for us as a staff. We wanted to reinforce how much the church really "cares" with our customer service, not just with our words. The only way to resolve the issues was to connect the multiple areas to operate as part of a larger family. Peter Drucker, management guru, makes the best case for it:

"The successful company is not the one with the most brains, but the most brains acting in concert."[2]

Getting our database in order and assembling a SuperTeam to protect it was the only responsible thing to do.[*]

Our SuperTeam meets for about an hour once a month to share stories that provide the needed context for data decisions and the systems that support them. They ask questions, clarify intentions and learn the benefits of relevant functionality. With a "shared ownership" mindset, they help discover how the pieces fit together and determine next steps to maximize operations churchwide, not just for one department. Most conversations are about topics of shared impact such as volunteers, staff responsiveness, event registrations, sensitive data, lists, reporting, check-in, and so on.

When the SuperTeam isn't meeting, each member operates as a power-user for his or her area of ministry. They watch for and address inconsistencies in data and reporting. They champion the team approach to increase the effectiveness of our whole organization, in every department.

Is somebody flying solo with your database today? Your database will only be as effective as the communication between departments. Set the stage for your SuperTeam strategy sooner rather than later. Ask that person flying solo to partner with just one other champion and operate as a team unit to put technology to work for you, not the other way around.[**]

---

[*] Our SuperTeam includes at least one person from each of these areas: arts, children and students, administrative support, IT, facilities, connections, counseling, finance, communications and missions.

[**] It's not an exact science. Our SuperTeam is in a constant fluid state, learning and adapting as we go. Your SuperTeam may only start out with two people. Ours did. Want to see how we evolved over time? It's in the back of the book.

NO MAN IS AN ISLAND

I heard a quote from John Donne— "No man is an island." In an organization, inter-dependencies exist among each other, resources and assets. We thrive when we have the ability to negotiate among these dependencies and find a middle ground where empowerment and decision-making align. To pull it off, though, we need to be clear about what we need from each other and realistic about the challenges that come with it.

This is an easier task if you start out by sharing the same mission across your organization. If we are all working toward the same goal, there will be less territorialism and more teamwork. Every ministry, every team, every employee, every volunteer leader should be looking at the same mission statement. Multiple, unique mission statements across a single organization create chaos and conflict.

Besides that, it breeds an environment where people operate in ministry silos. You know what I'm talking about, right? The connections department runs its own campaign and doesn't see what's being communicated by the volunteer areas, the missions area, the student ministry area, the children's area, the men's and women's ministry teams, the pastor, and others. The missions department does its own thing. The student leaders do their own thing. And, the pattern repeats throughout the whole church.

The result? **Individual departments end up competing against each other with a carnival communication style trying to out-yell or out-explain.**

One mission statement transcends specific departments to unify the whole. Our mission statement at Granger is "Helping people take their next step toward Christ...together." That mission statement applies to every ministry. It doesn't mean the mission statement action steps can't be tailored to a specific audience. But, everybody is working toward the same goal, like-minded, maintaining alignment. "Helping students take their next step toward Christ...together." "Helping women take their next step toward Christ...together." "Helping people afraid of dogs take their next steps toward Christ...together."

We are all on the same page. No man is an island.

WHO IS IN CHARGE OF WHAT?

I frequently get questions about what our Communications Department "controls." People want to see how our boxes and lines are drawn. It is a hard question to answer because we don't have hard lines and boxes. We need a hierarchy for obvious reasons, but our daily operations don't run linear in assembly-line format.

The team culture here is all about shared ownership. We are not segregated departments, but we're not all morphed into *one* department with *one* person in charge of it all either. There are continuous conversations happening between key stakeholders who are intentional about collaboration and cross training. Although it might be easier if everyone stayed in his or her own area, it just wouldn't be as effective. It's one more thing we have learned from our senior pastor, Mark Beeson.*

Sometimes you have to trade efficiency for effectiveness.

I'll attempt to explain how we divide up supporting communication responsibilities at Granger using a very loose football analogy.

- As Pastor of Creative Arts, Butch Whitmire and his performing arts teams are responsible for executing the plays on the auditorium platform. That affects the vocal team, the band, technical arts, media, drama, and so on.

- As Pastor of Connections, Mark Waltz and his teams are responsible for executing the plays for the best

---

* If you're thinking, "She sure has quoted Mark Beeson a lot in this section," you're right. There's nobody I've learned more from about the effectiveness of a successful team than him. He gets buy-in and brings the glue to keep people connected to the vision. He can herd cats and make them feel like lions. Rawr. You can learn from him, too, at MarkBeeson.com.

environments. That affects events, care and counseling, guest services, retail, and so on.

- As Communications Director, I am the coach responsible for anything you read, touch or click beyond the auditorium stage. That affects promotions, print materials, the Web site, IT, etc.

Each department has a leader that acts as a quarterback to carry the vision, run the plays and keep the ball moving down the field on a daily basis. The rest of the staff team has specific positions to play in the game but can be moved around, depending on the situational landscape.

There's a lot of overlap among us, but we're all protecting the same mission, vision and values so it works well. For direction, our senior leadership team creates one big idea worksheet* for each series. Our individual jobs are easier, and our efforts are more unified because nobody operates independently trying to "define" what is communicated. Everything is tied back to the big idea worksheet—it unifies promotions, the service production, the scheduled programs out of the weekend, and so on. Once we know what the message is going to be for the weekend—we all run our respective teams to protect, support and extend that message.

Of course, at any time, we may make mid-play course corrections, yielding to the direction from the team owners, Mark Beeson and Tim Stevens, our senior and executive pastors. They care about the team running the plays as well as the fans.

I told you it was a loose analogy. But it works.

---

* Of course there's a sample for you in the "back of the book." I can't believe you even asked.

THINK IT OVER

The responsibility of buy-in—bring the glue.

☐ Where are my loyalties misplaced? What changes can we make to prioritize people over policy?

☐ Are we ineffective trying to get the word out *about* our organization because we fail to equip the people *in* our organization? What tools and coaching can we provide to help unify words and actions?

☐ Do we have people in place who can effectively balance individual needs and corporate needs? Are we maximizing that skill set to maximize the benefits of a team?

☐ What things are we promoting as an organization that foster silo ministry? Is it individual mission statements? Separate budgets? Individual marketing plans? What can we do with our systems and conversations to eliminate a competitive "us versus them" spirit between departments?

chapter 15

GETTING FROM HERE TO THERE

Implementing a communication strategy happens through a series of steps that build on each other. But, the concept is all-encompassing, and the task at hand is so big. It's hard to know where to begin. After all, you have a job to do, and the ministry around you will not allow for a hard reboot—you can't just stop the bus and rearrange everything. However, you could use some handles, next steps and tools to help evaluate and organize the internal chaos. Some places to start and some early wins can help.

MAKE TIME FOR CONVERSATIONS

If your job has anything to do with communications, then you need to look at your schedule and see how much space you are leaving for *conversations*. (**Hint: everybody's job has something to do with communications.**)

Now, I'll just bet there are a few of you out there who just read that and have this in the thought bubble above your head:

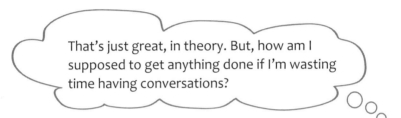

That's just great, in theory. But, how am I supposed to get anything done if I'm wasting time having conversations?

If you're not leaving time on your calendar—the white space—for impromptu conversations with the people you work with, then don't expect to see organizational and relational change anytime soon. You see, momentum advances over time through a series of conversations; it is not a one-happy-chat or email event.

If you're still thinking to yourself:

I can't afford the time for that.

I say, you can't afford not to. Every conversation you invest in on the front end makes the next project go smoother. At the end of the day, it's all in our perspective, isn't it?

Mark Beeson talked to a group of church leaders about what is needed to promote forward movement, progress and next steps as an organization. Interestingly, everything he shared starts with an individual's personal habits, not his or her tasks.

You can't get what you could have until you let go of what you do have. We all need to work on our:

- **Attitude**—without this, you will hurt yourself.

- **Relationships**—without these, others will hurt you.

- **Persistence**—without this, problems will defeat you.

- **Priorities**—without these, the insignificant will hamper you.

- **Credibility**—without this, no one will follow you.

You in? I thought so. I know you can do it. Just be prepared. There will be times when you lose momentum and experience reversal of hard-won gains. Along the way, some days you will feel strong, and some days you will feel defeated. Stay the course and keep working on your personal habits. Get what you *could* have by letting go of what you *do* have.

LEADING CHANGE

People need people. They bring out the best and worst in us, don't they?

When it comes to our jobs, our neighborhoods, our communities and the lasting impact we make on this life, significance cannot happen without people. **And, growth can't happen without change. But, change makes people whickety whack.** [*]

Author Eric Hoffer said, "Every new adjustment is a crisis in self-esteem." Have you ever been there? Quit lying. I know you have.

Awareness of this reality is where successful change management comes in. To lead change, you have to be conscientious about leading up, sideways and inside. I got some advice from a very smart leader I know [**] about this topic. I've taken what he shared with me and added some ideas of my own to create the following list.

- **Build alliances.** Add some people to your trust pool who have not always agreed with you. Adopt a no-turf policy and treat people as partners.

- **Be realistic.** Old habits and existing problems are not easily solved. Don't give yourself or others false hope pretending they will be.

- **Go to the source.** Rather than make grand assumptions and quick decisions, make a point of visiting others where they work. See how they operate. Judge firsthand what the problems are before you attempt to develop solutions.

---

[*] You can quote me on that. Go ahead. W-h-i-c-k-e-t-y w-h-a-c-k.
[**] Ladies and gentlemen, meet my husband—Mark Meyer. He has more smart insight that provokes personal and group excellence at maximeyer.blogspot.com.

- **Go unrecognized**. Look for ways to help others succeed. Find ways to make them look like rock stars, even if that is not in your job description.

- **Be different**. It's normal to blame, complain and let others worry about fixing problems. Don't be normal. Make it about others, not yourself.

If you are trying to lead change in any organization and influence any group of people—students, churches, businesses, communities, a family—in today's uncertain times, this list applies to you.

WHERE DO I START?

One of the biggest myths I consistently hear is, "We don't have excellence in church communications because we don't have the money for it." That is not a reason; it's an excuse. I hate it when I hear people say that.

A small budget is not a hurdle to jump. It does not prevent you from WOWing your guest and it does not restrict you from adding value. I read* about the budget restraints Steven Spielberg faced when he was shooting *Jaws*. He was just getting started in the business and didn't have a dream budget. He wanted to film an incredibly lifelike mechanical great white shark attacking and consuming weak humans en masse. The problem? An incredibly lifelike mechanical great white shark was incredibly expensive. So what did he do? He didn't make a bad movie and blame lack of money for it. He had to think of something else. Something creative. Something cheap. He decided to shoot the unsuspecting swimmers from the *shark's* point of view (with scary music), and it resulted in a classic.

Resist the temptation to blame lack of financial resources for the reason you can't make improvements. Here are some things you can do right now to improve your church communications with no additional money:

- **Have conversations.** Lots of them. Help coach the people you work with to stop thinking brochures and start thinking about objectives and customer service.

- **Create a style guide.** A consistent stylistic approach will have a positive impact on the overall excellence of your church.

---

* I first read the story in Biz Stone's book, *Blogging*. I bet you didn't know Biz is one of the co-founders of Twitter.

- **Identify your specific audience.** You need to know who you're talking to before you know how to say it.

- **Document your communication values.** What is the method and context of your environment? Find out and write it down.

- **Outline a strategy.** Determine what is communicated, in what priority, using what vehicles. Not *all* news is appropriate for the *entire* church.

- **Reduce emotional overload.** Create less and say more. Look at everything you're creating and find something to cut. Look at the number of words (or pages) in your bulletin, and edit them down.

- **Implement an official proofing team and process.** Have a group of volunteers review everything for accuracy and consistency before it's printed or distributed.

- **Assemble a group of consumer advocates (or secret shoppers).** This team of critical thinkers can experience your materials *from the shark's perspective* and provide input into what's working and what isn't. Have them attend the service as an outsider and provide feedback about the things you can't see yourself.

This works if you are a church of 10 or 10,000. Either way. Money or not, this list is a great place to start. You have resources. You just need to use them in better ways.*

---

* You can find samples for the audience profile, communication values, promotional priorities and a few sample pages from our style guide in the "back of the book."

PICK UP YOUR BATON

Last year when I was on vacation, I had the opportunity to hear speaker Christine Caine[1] from Australia deliver a message at Healing Place Church in Louisiana. How is *that* for a blending of cultures—a girl from Indiana listening to a girl from Australia speak to a group of people in the Bayou? The message struck a chord, and it has set off a continued reverb in me that hasn't stopped since I've heard it. It keeps coming back to me. I think it was important. I'll do my best to paraphrase.

She talked about how, in relay races, it doesn't matter how fast, how big, how strong or how fantastic you run your leg of the race—an entire team can be disqualified because one person doesn't hand the baton over right.[*] To drive the point home, she replayed how the American team lost their race in the 2004 Athens Olympics. They had the fastest qualifying team in the women's 4 x 100 final. They should have won. Everybody knew they were going to win. But, guess what? They lost. All because of the baton exchange.[**]

God uses your life as part of a bigger plan. This race is not an individual sprint. The church is interdependent—running together on a relay team. So what are we to do?

- **Strip down.** Runners strip themselves of any unnecessary weights so they can run unencumbered. What do we need to strip? The baton exchange between Saul and David should have been seamless, but Saul didn't deal with issues of his heart, so it became a complex affair.

[*] In case you forgot, remember Paul likens our life to a relay race in 1 Corinthians 9:24–27.

[**] There's a 20-meter exchange zone where it's legal to hand over the baton. If you don't hand it over the right way, the whole team gets disqualified. During the race, between runners 2 (Marion Jones) and 3 (Lauren Williams), the race was lost because of a bad exchange.

- **Look at the team**. Don't forget others have come before you. You had better remember this because if you don't, you just might forget there are still others to come after you. It's not just about the here and now, but about your part of something bigger that God's been doing throughout all of eternity. We can lose sight of what's going on if we don't remember we didn't just arrive. A whole generation that came before you paid a massive price for you to be here. And, others will come after you, counting on you to carry the baton to them.

- **Take your place**. Everything will take longer than you think. In a relay, runner #4 doesn't get his nose out of joint when he doesn't get to run with a baton when the gun goes off. He understands there is a process that happens before he gets the baton. In churches, in life, God sees beyond what we do. He sees runner #4 in position years before he or she is ever there. Too often though, we get out of place, and we will never be in position for the baton because we didn't take our place at the beginning.

- **Play it out daily**. It is not the responsibility of politicians, the media or educational systems to carry the baton and leave a legacy for this generation. It's our responsibility, and God is trusting us to carry the baton. What does this look like every 24 hours in our seemingly insignificant life? It doesn't matter if you're a full-time homemaker, a corporate CEO, in manufacturing, a teacher, a student, a librarian or a doctor. Every normal daily decision counts. Don't cheat, quit or give in to shortcuts others accept—don't drop the baton.

- **Endure**. Things get hard. You'll get tired. The heat will turn up. You'll want to give up. Though we are confronting great obstacles and hurdles as a church (and individuals), this is not a time to give up. It's a time to endure and get our eyes off our temporal circumstances because there is a bigger picture. It only takes one generation to drop the baton and sever the next generation. Don't be surprised when a generation ends up living as if they came from nothing and live for no reason, and they're going nowhere when that's all they've been taught.

- **Go back and pick up your baton**. We are all interdependent on each other. It doesn't matter if you can run like Marion Jones because unless you run your 100 well, cross the line and exchange the baton successfully, then the whole team loses. Get back in your lane, take your place and start running your race to finish your course. If you dropped a baton, go back and pick it up yourself. Don't wait for somebody else to do it. Jesus gives us forgiveness for our past, a brand new start today and hope for our future. So, don't waste time feeling like a loser if you dropped a baton. Just go back and pick it up.

We are here for a purpose. The baton is in our hands.

THINK IT OVER

The responsibility of buy-in—getting from here to there.

- [ ] Is something holding me back from the change I need in me, so I can change my team? Is it unresolved heart issues: anger, fear, insecurity, jealousy and so on? Or, is it another type of weight: culture, tradition, expectations or out-dated habits?

- [ ] If God looks at the twenty-first century and says, "Who was the church?" what will be my reply? What will happen to this nation on my watch? What personal and organizational habits are status quo that I am willing to change?

- [ ] What *could* I have if I let go of what I *do* have?

- [ ] Am I conscientious about leading up, sideways and inside? How can I improve? Am I reacting to my own self-esteem crisis or helping others through theirs?

- [ ] Do I use lack of money as an excuse not to do better?

- [ ] Do I approach problems like a hit-and-run car accident, only identifying the problem without following through with the possible solutions and approaches to get there?

now what?

BACK OF THE BOOK

If I were you, I'd be looking for some practical help for taking my next steps after reading this book. That's what the *Back of the Book* is for. You'll find a variety of links, lists and examples of stuff I've found useful along the way. I've also included some sample documents we've used at Granger to coordinate communications. Some are current and others are from the archive, but they might help inspire your own ideas for the change you are leading. You can download full, editable versions of any of these sample documents at WiredChurches.com. And, here's a test just to see if you're still reading: to download a free copy of the Communications Manual, add it to your cart, go to check out and enter **LESSCLUTTER** in the coupon code field.

KEM'S TOP 10 READING LIST

1. *Simply Strategic Series*, Tony Morgan & Tim Stevens

2. *First Impressions & Lasting Impressions*, Mark Waltz

3. *All Marketers are Liars*, Seth Godin

4. *You Don't Need a Title to be a Leader*, Mark Sanborn

5. *Be Our Guest*, The Disney Institute

6. *The 22 Immutable Laws of Branding*, Al & Laura Ries

7. *The Brand Gap*, Marty Neumeier

8. *Love is the Killer App*, Tim Sanders

9. *Seven Practices of Effective Ministry*, Andy Stanley

10. *The Blogging Church*, Brian Bailey & Terry Storch

A FEW GRANGER BLOGS

- **Mark Beeson | Senior Pastor**
  markbeeson.com

- **Tim Stevens | Executive Pastor**
  leadingsmart.com

- **Rob Wegner | Pastor of Life Mission**
  robwegner.org

- **Mark Waltz | Pastor of Connections**
  becausepeoplematter.com

- **Butch Whitmire | Pastor of Creative Arts**
  butchwhitmire.com

- **Jeff Bell | Elkhart Campus Pastor**
  elkhartpastor.com

- **Jason Miller| Pastor of Worship
  and College Age Ministries**
  commonjason.com

- **Jason Powell | IT Director**
  jpowell.blogs.com

- **Daryl McMullen | Web Director**
  webdrivenchurch.com

- **Dave Moore | Finance Director**
  mooreforthemoney.blogspot.com

- **DC Curry | Director of Student Ministries**
  currystew.org

- **Kathy Guy | Director of Community**
  becauserelationshipsmatter.net

- **Jack Magruder | Director of Life Mission**
  smartzombie.blogspot.com

SAMPLING OF THE GRANGER
AUDIENCE MINDSET

- Primarily unchurched

- Educated

- Likes his/her job

- Enjoys what is "different" and "unique"; innovators on the edge

- Values creativity

- Likes the "buzz" of a big crowd, but intimacy of friends

- Searching for truth; for something more in this life

- Doesn't want all the answers; "Get me thinking, but don't tell me what to think"

- All about the "experience"

- Skeptical of institutions, government and "organized" religion

- Independent thinkers; value individual expression

- Prefers the casual and informal over the formal; "be who you are"

- Over-extended in both time and money

- Consumer mindset; accustomed to being served

- Wants to do the right thing; on their own terms

This is who we are called to serve. And, it's this profile we use to define and prioritize message series, graphics, music, furniture, promotions, copy and everything in between.

COMMUNICATING CHANGE FOR BUY-IN

Jason Powell, our IT Director, has implemented quite a few new systems and I appreciate how he communicates changes along the way. Here is an excerpt from one of Jason's all-staff emails.

Why do we need new technology guidelines? To maximize empowerment and minimize liability. These guidelines allow you to do what you want to do without blowing yourself (or the church) up in the process.

Why do I have to run my technology purchases through you when I'm paying for it out of my budget anyway? Dude, that's a great question. We don't need to approve your every move, but face it...we're always a stakeholder. Even if you buy that phone or laptop with money out of your own piggy bank, you'll end up using it at work and that affects all of us. Go through IT and it will increase the church's buying power and support capacity. Cut us out of the conversation, and it will ending up hurting you and the rest of the team. Remember "call before you dig"? It's like that.

Why do we all have the same computers? Equipment standardization across an organization of our size is like a secret weapon. Yes, you may lose your ability to express your individuality through the computer on your desk, but you'll also lose a mountain of technical barriers. Because we're standardized, our machines are compatible with each other; we can swap pieces and parts on the spot with low to no cost. Plus, our support responsiveness is like BAM! because our depth of knowledge makes us experts on one main platform. What does this mean to you? Less downtime and more productivity (believe me, you'll appreciate this when - not if - your computer goes down).

ALL CHURCH COMMUNICATION VALUES

The foundational why behind the how we communicate.

Granger Community Church
All-Church Communication Values

OUR CHURCH COMMUNICATION WILL...

- Reinforce that we are a unified church working toward a common vision, not a federation of sub-ministries.

- Be driven from the outside-in. That is, there will be a heavier emphasis communicating to those in the outside circles (community and crowd), and a progressively lighter emphasis toward those in the inner circles (congregation, committed and core).

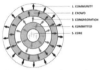

- Capitalize on our strength. Most people will connect to GCC for the first time through a weekend service. Therefore, most of our communication resources will be expended on inviting people to the weekend service, and then helping them take their next step from there.

- Not be fair, but instead will be appropriate based on ministry priorities. This means that "equal time" is not valued or considered.

- Focus on the needs of our guests, not the needs of our ministries.

- Ask more questions than we answer; drawing people into the content we have to offer –allowing them to absorb and seek on their own terms.

We do this...

- Deliver excellence in timeliness, accuracy, design, layout and ease of use.

- Be simple and clear, eliminating unnecessary fluff or complicated content.

- Always be in a language, style and method that is visible and understandable to the first-time guest.

- Be designed so that it reduces the noise in people's lives and eliminates competition between ministries. Too much information can be just as dangerous as not enough. Therefore, we will provide the basic information for people to easily scan.

Instead of this...

- Be sustainable. We won't launch a deliverable (e.g., newsletter or web page) if we don't have the systems and personnel to maintain it with excellence.

- Actively balance inspiration and information. Therefore, everything will be evaluated in context of the church; not just a ministry audience.

How we communicate with each other and our audience brings our values to life. By protecting these values, we are able to help people take their next step towards Christ through excellent, easy-to-use and easy-to-maintain communication tools. The objective is to simplify everything our audience sees, to make their life easier and more rewarding in every interaction with our church and ministries.

ALL CHURCH PROMOTIONS PRIORITIES

The foundational what gets promoted when, where and why.

Granger Community Church
Branding, Emphasis & Deliverables

BRANDING Our brand is the overall identity for the church. It resonates through our design, our events, the attitude of our staff and volunteers, locations and the overall consistency of the experience we deliver. Done right, our brand has the power of "meaning"—individual departments speaking as part of one family.

To make that brand connection stronger, we're organized as a 'branded house' (not a 'house of brands'). In other words, **Granger Community Church is the brand** and all of our activities are an extension of that brand; *individual events and ministries don't stand alone.*

EMPHASIS AND DELIVERABLES

HIGH: The 20% that affects 80% of the audience; this week Granger and Elkhart, next steps out of the weekend and all-church events.

Sample events:
- Weekend series (children, students and adults)
- 1ˢᵗ Wednesday and Journey Bible classes
- Attend an event, volunteer and find a group:
  - 2ⁿᵈ Saturday, Volunteer Expo, Men's/ Women' retreats
  - Starting Point, Turning Point and Express groups
  - Core Classes and Budget class during a money series
  - Men's and women's retreats
- Baptism and dedication
- Campaign news

Sample promotional vehicles:
- Platform announcements
- The Feed
- GCCwired.com home page
- Custom media
- Direct mail
- Enewsletter feature
- Custom graphics

MEDIUM: Mid-sized events that affect a large group, but not 80% of the audience.

Sample events:
- Budget class not tied to a money series
- Campus work day
- Job openings

Sample promotional vehicles:
- Bulletin
- Pre-service slide
- 3x5 postcard or fact sheet

LIGHT: Niche news or small volume events

Sample events:
- Scrapbooking
- Golf outing
- Team meeting

Sample promotional vehicles:
- Events page on GCCwired.com
- Personal invites
- Conversations

ALL CHURCH PROMOTIONS PROCESS

This is a big picture document that helps us see, at a glance, what happens when for series promotions.

ALL CHURCH PROMOTIONS PROCESS

One year in advance -- Senior Management Team outlines series for the year.

Three to six months in advance -- Senior Management Team determines actual series name/theme.

One to two months in advance -- Big Idea is communicated to staff, teams, etc. Communications and Creative Arts brainstorm big idea and then break into respective areas. Communications focusing on graphics, promotions and marketing. Creative arts focusing on programming and internal supporting media.

One month in advance -- Communications team coordinates the series promotional piece (postcard) with volunteer designer and proofing team and provides graphics/theme to Creative Arts team.

One month in advance (if applicable) -- Send news release to local media promoting the event. Please note: this is only applicable if it's a newsworthy series and adds value to our community.

Two week in advance -- After the postcard is finalized, communications team requests graphic designer to deliver the following elements to be used in other promotional pieces of the church:
1. High-resolution square image for print bulletin cover. (300 dpi)
2. B/W version of series title graphic JPG file for use on Granger Notes.
3. Color version of series title graphic JPG file for back of postcard.
4. Low-resolution JPG image for Web (458 x 234 pixels and 662 x 380 pixels)
5. Thumbnail JPG image for Web and Enews (exactly 186 x 95 pixels)
6. Original photoshop layered file. (720 x 480 pixels or 8.5 x 5.5 in) to Arts team
7. All relevant fonts.
8. Graphics for a banner to hang in the Atrium, plus bottom 'Hello' -- if needed.

Communications team alerts relevant parties of their location to use the pieces they need. (Web, Enews, Media, etc.)

Two weeks in advance -- Postcard is inserted in the bulletin (encouraging people to use to invite a friend) and mailed to GCC database. Media Trailer is shown in service.

One week in advance -- Web Director gets Web elements and updates: Current Series page, any flash stories and Evites. Sends live link to Communications Coordinator for proofing.

One week in advance -- Upcoming series is promoted in the Enewsletter.

Week of series -- Communications team coordinates bulletin with printer (use graphic designer from printer). During series, pre-print 4-color bulletin shells. Weekly overprint current information in black ink. Bulletin coordination finalized on Wednesday with delivery on Friday.

ALL CHURCH PROMOTION PROCESS

	1 year	6 months	5 months	4 months	3 months	2 months	1 month	3 weeks	2 weeks	1 week	Kickoff week	During series
	Series Outlined	Series Defined										
						Theme Communicated to Staff, Teams, etc.						
							Series Promotional Pieces Press Releases if applicable		Delivery of Graphic Elements	Postcard Inserted in Bulletin, Enewsletter Series Promotion	Bulletin Shells Printed	Weekly Bulletin Printed
										Web Page Updated		

Legend: Senior Management Team | Communications Team | Staff | Web Team

COMMUNICATIONS & PROMOTIONS PROCESS

ONE STEP. Enter EVERYTHING into EventU by Monday noon. That's it.

- This applies for on- and off-campus events. If it's happening as part a of Granger ministry, it counts.

- When you enter your event (or meeting, or class, etc.) into EventU, it starts a domino effect, impacting multiple teams across multiple disciplines. Potentially, it affects the church calendar, facility space, database structure, technical support, check-in, guest services, promotions, etc. The more thorough the information you include, the better equipped the supporting teams are to serve your needs. Even if you don't think it's relevant, the impact of your event will be stronger the more you share. It provides the background context for the different teams to "do their thing" in tandem with you.

- If you've created any materials (e.g., handouts, postcard, letter, etc.), attach it in EventU for proofing (allow 24 hour turnaround).

WE'LL TAKE CARE OF THE REST. The Communications team will help create the conditions for getting your project complete.

- They'll facilitate collaboration through all phases of the project (from concept to completion) to maximize all required resources (creative, calendar, technical, web, etc.) They'll assemble the right project team for you, pulling the right stakeholders together at the right time to help accomplish your objectives.

- They'll serve as your eyes and ears, protecting the various touch points to guarantee everyone involved is telling the same story, providing the same experience.

- Depending on the scope of your event or project, they'll coordinate the tasks and people associated with, but not limited to:
  - Platform announcements and pre-service slides
  - Bulletin (content, inserts and or stub)
  - Enewsletter (content and links)
  - GCCwired.com
  - WiredChurches.com
  - Registration (online and off)
  - Volunteer Hot Opportunities (online & VolunTOUR script)
  - Media relations
  - Kiosk support
  - Signage
  - Reporting
  - And more...

SPEAKING SCHEDULE FOR THE YEAR

Our Executive Pastor provides this outline to use as a tool at the beginning of every year. It's a working document that starts as a high level outline (major themes/date chunks) and becomes more detailed as the year goes on. This resource point drives next steps.

2009 Speaking Schedule

Date	Day	Comments	Speaker	Topic
1/4/09	Sunday		Beeson	Ask Your Question
1/11/09	Sunday	Food Drop 1/10; SMT Retreat 1/12-16	HOST Beeson	From Garage to Glory (LARRY JONES)
1/18/09	Sunday		Beeson	Help Wanted: Surviving Tough Times
1/25/09	Sunday		Beeson	Help Wanted: Surviving Tough Times
2/1/09	Sunday	Beeson Orlando 2/1-9	Beeson	Help Wanted: Surviving Tough Times
2/8/09	Sunday	Beeson Orlando 2/1-9; UMC Pastors Houston 2/12-13	Wegner	Go Fish
2/15/09	Sunday		Beeson	Go Fish
2/22/09	Sunday	Willow Summit Strategy 2/23-24; Beeson Tucson 2/26-3/5	Beeson	Go Fish
3/1/09	Sunday	Beeson Tucson 2/26-3/5	Wegner	Go Fish
3/8/09	Sunday		Beeson	BIG DEAL: Sex for Sale
3/15/09	Sunday		Beeson	BIG DEAL: Sex for Sale
3/22/09	Sunday		Wegner	BIG DEAL: Sex for Sale
3/29/09	Sunday		Wegner	BIG DEAL: Sex for Sale
4/5/09	Sunday	Palm Sunday; PHM Spring Break 4/6-10	Jason	Palm Sunday Focus
4/12/09	Sunday	Easter Weekend	Beeson	Purpose Driven Series
4/19/09	Sunday	Beeson Union Chapel Staff 4/23-25	Beeson	Purpose Driven Series
4/26/09	Sunday		Wegner	Purpose Driven Series
5/3/09	Sunday	Leadership Live 5/6-7	Wegner	Purpose Driven Series
5/10/09	Sunday	Mother's Day	Beeson	Purpose Driven Series
5/17/09	Sunday		Beeson	STAND-ALONE
5/24/09	Sunday	PHM Final Day 5/22; Memorial Day 5/25	Wegner	STAND-ALONE
5/31/09	Sunday		Beeson	STAND-ALONE
6/7/09	Sunday	Wegner India June ALL	HOST Beeson	One Prayer Beeson VIDEO
6/14/09	Sunday	Wegner India June ALL; Camp Adventure #1 6/15-20	HOST Jason	One Prayer Guest VIDEO
6/21/09	Sunday	Wegner India June ALL; UMC Conf 6/24-27; Jason ND 6/22-7/3	HOST Waltz	One Prayer Guest VIDEO
6/28/09	Sunday	Wegner India June ALL	HOST Bell	One Prayer Guest VIDEO
7/5/09	Sunday	July 4th Weekend; Camp Adventure #2 7/6-11	Beeson	JULY 4th FOCUS
7/12/09	Sunday		Beeson	Sand Traps Series
7/19/09	Sunday		Beeson	Sand Traps Series
7/26/09	Sunday		Laurent	Sand Traps Series
8/2/09	Sunday		Beeson	Sand Traps Series
8/9/09	Sunday	Beeson Fishing? 8/8-8/16	Jason	STAND ALONE - MUSIC/MESSAGE
8/16/09	Sunday	Beeson Fishing? 8/8-8/16	Wegner	Prep for Big Deal / Baptism
8/23/09	Sunday	PHM Begins 8/19; Beeson Phil Wedding 8/22	Wegner	Prep for Big Deal / Baptism
8/30/09	Sunday	Beeson Colorado UMC 8/31-9/2	Wegner	Prep for Big Deal / Baptism
9/6/09	Sunday	Labor Day 9/7	Beeson	Prep for Big Deal / Baptism
9/13/09	Sunday		Beeson	Big Deal Series
9/20/09	Sunday	Innovate 9/23-25	Beeson	Big Deal Series
9/27/09	Sunday		Laurent	Big Deal Series
10/4/09	Sunday		Beeson	Big Deal Series
10/11/09	Sunday		Beeson	Fall Series
10/18/09	Sunday		Jason	Fall Series
10/25/09	Sunday		Jason	Fall Series
11/1/09	Sunday		Beeson	Fall Series
11/8/09	Sunday		Wegner	Wegner Series
11/15/09	Sunday	Indiana Gun 11/15-30	Wegner	Wegner Series
11/22/09	Sunday	Indiana Gun 11/15-30; Thanksgiving 11/26	Wegner	Wegner Series
11/29/09	Sunday	Indiana Gun 11/15-30; Wegner India 11/29-12/9	Jason	Wegner Series (Thanksgiving)
12/6/09	Sunday	Indiana Muzzle 12/5-20; Wegner India 11/29-12/9	Beeson	Christmas
12/13/09	Sunday	Indiana Muzzle 12/5-20	Beeson	Christmas
12/20/09	Sunday		Beeson	Christmas
12/27/09	Sunday	Xmas Eve Thursday	Laurent	STAND ALONE

PROMOTIONS OUTLINE

This is an abbreviated snapshot of major events we've got planned for the year. The Communications Department uses this document to cross reference with the speaking schedule to coordinate major series and with events. A lot of times, it's an at-a-glance snapshot. It's helpful to keep in front of us as we're promoting and packaging any events, programs, groups, etc. The more opportunities we have to communicate these things as next steps out of a series, the more clear the path becomes to our audience and the more successful these events and programs are. For example, when we're in the middle of a money series in January, that'd be a great time to schedule the financial freedom course (not during the sex series in July). In other words, we schedule ministry events on the calendar to meet and match all-church programming, not individual ministry team plans.

2009 Promotions Schedule

Date	Day	Speaker	Series	Message Title	Big Idea	Next Steps/Resources
1/4/09	Sunday	Beeson	Just Go Ahead and Ask	Ask	Text Mark Your Questions	Food Drop
1/11/09	Sunday	HOST Beeson	From Garage to Glory	Larry Jones	Food Drop	2nd Saturday
1/18/09	Sunday	Beeson	Help Wanted: Surviving Tough Times	I've Never Seen it This Bad	Choose Perspective (choose to see things with an eternal perspective; choose to keep your attitude positive).	Journey Bible Classes continue this week • View Point bible study groups launch this Monday, Jan 19 • Turning Point launches Monday, Jan 26
1/25/09	Sunday	Beeson	Help Wanted: Surviving Tough Times	I Think We Might Lose Everything	Choose Simplicity	• Monday Nights are Group Night at GCC: • Turning Point launches this Monday, Jan 26 • Starting Point for Marrieds – Mon, Feb 9
2/1/09	Sunday	Beeson	Help Wanted: Surviving Tough Times	I Think It Will Get Worse Before It Gets Better	Choose Generosity	• First Wednesday – this Wed, Feb 4 • Journey bible classes • Financial Peace University – Monday, Feb 23 • (New series begins next week)
2/8/09	Sunday	Wegner	Go Fish	Fishers of...	Remember where you came from... what was it like? Jesus calls us from where we were to be fishers of men. (w/Mark B brief video message)	• Journey Bible Classes- 2.11 • Financial Peace U – 2.23 • Second Saturday – 2.14 • Starting Point, marrieds-2.9 (if room to put in FEED)
2/15/09	Sunday	Beeson	Go Fish	Muddy Water	People need to know they matter. People need someONE to invest. to invite. People need Jesus.	• Journey Bible Classes – Wednesday evening – 6:30 • Financial Peace U- 2.23
2/22/09	Sunday	Beeson	Go Fish	Fishing Buddies	What doesn't work: cultural realities that frame the worldview of our friends. Engaging personal conversations that communicate care.	• * See note below re: Beyond I Do... • Financial Peace U – 2.23 • First Wednesday – 3.4
3/1/09	Sunday	Wegner	Go Fish	Fish Guts	Why the local church partnership matters in personal evangelism.	• First Wednesday – 3.4 • Journey Bible Classes – 3.11

SERIES PROMOTION

This is the documentation we use in our communications department as the how-to sheet and steps we follow for series promotions every 3-6 weeks. It's a checklist we use for quality control, training, memory supplement, etc.

SERIES PROMOTION DEVELOPMENT

1. Executive Pastor sends "concept" email to graphic designer with CC: to Communications Director and Communications Manager.

2. Communications Manager works to maintain deadline schedule and get approval from Executive Pastor on final concept.

3. Executive Pastor is out of the loop once approval is granted. Deadlines with series promotion checklist (containing the following elements) is established by Communications Manager and sent to series graphic designer.

250

   a) High-res horizontal image for print postcard. (300 dpi)
   b) High-res vertical image for print bulletin cover. (300 dpi)
   c) B/W version of series title graphic (JPG) for use on Granger Notes.
   d) Color version of series title graphic (JPG) for back of postcard.
      (If applicable, also get other individual art elements that are used on back of postcard.)
   e) Low-res JPG image for Web. (458 x 234 pixels)
   f) Thumbnail JPG image for Web. (186 x 95 pixels)
   g) Photoshop layered file. (At least 458 x 234 pixels)
   h) All relevant fonts.
   i) Flash script for above graphic (458 x 234 pixels). Note: don't add sound in Flash script.

4. Communications coordinates proofing of postcard elements with the proofing team.

5. When elements are posted on the web directory, Communications alerts relevant parties of their location to use the pieces they need.

6. Web Director gets web graphics and updates Current Weekend Series Page/Evites/Enews. Sends live link to Communications Coordinator for proofing.

BIG IDEA WORKSHEET

This is probably the most comprehensive snapshot of a series. It's an extension of the Speaking Schedule and it's what we use to write the copy, creative concepts, prioritize promotions, etc.

251

REELDATING

Week	Title	Big Idea	Next Steps (in bulletin)	Key Promotions—from platform (No more than 2 each weekend)
Aug 26/27 Beeson	**Hitch** When do you make a commitment, and what does it look like after you do?	A commitment should be based on your values. Once you make the commitment, your behavior should change.	○ Core classes: Sept 5 ○ Starting Point for Singles Only: Sept 11 ○ Baptism: Sept 10	○ Core 101-401: Saturday, Sept 5 ○ Baptism: Sept 10 ○ Singles Starting Point: Sept 11
Sept 2/3 Beeson	**Meet the Parents** In today's crazy world, how do you prepare your kid for dating?	Prepare your kids well so they will have great relationships leading toward a great marriage.	○ Core classes: Sept 5 ○ Baptism: Sept 10 ○ Starting Point for Singles Only: Sept 11 ○ Second Saturday: Sept 9	○ Core 101-401: Sept 5 ○ Baptism: Sept 10 ○ Singles Starting Point: Sept 11
Sept 9/10 Beeson	**A Lot Like Love** We're just friends. Or are we? How do we start dating without letting things get out of hand?	Principles that will take you from a friendship toward marriage without messing up. (Includes appropriate boundaries).	○ Baptism: Sunday! ○ Starting Point for Singles Only: Sept 11	○ Baptism: Sunday! ○ Singles Starting Point: this Monday, Sept 11
Sept 16/17 Beeson	**Mr. & Mrs. Smith** Just because you are married doesn't mean you should stop dating.	Dating gives you the time that is required to maintain faithfulness in your marriage.	○ Starting Point for Married Couples Only: Oct 2	○ Married Couples Starting Point: Oct 2 ○ Next series: (Fall Launch)
Sept 23/24 Laurent	**How to Lose a Guy in 10 Days** What are the signs that you are in a relationship that is taking you down?	Don't enter a relationship thinking you can change the other person. Determine your non-negotiables and don't compromise.	○ Starting Point for Married Couples Only: Oct 2 ○ Men's Retreat: Oct 13/14	○ Married Couples Starting Point: Oct 2 ○ Men's Retreat: Oct 13/14 ○ Next series: (Fall Launch)

Let's face it—everyone has either been on a date or will be soon. Yes, even you married couples. Isn't it about time that the church starts a conversation on this topic? After all, the Bible is incredibly practical and has so much to help us in our relationships. How do you recognize Mr. Right? How do you see past the first impression to discover who's really behind that smile? Or how do you find a mate when you can't even find a date? And if you're married your dating reality may seem as illusive. How do you keep the romance alive? And how do you help your kids avoid some of the same mistakes you made in your dating days?

Join us at Granger Community Church for some straight talk about sex, dating and romance – whether you're married, single, single again or a student. For five weeks, we'll look at the advice of Hollywood and compare it to the teachings of the Bible.

STYLE GUIDE

A few sample pages of the one we created for Granger are included here, but you can download the full version from WiredChurches.com, edit it and make it your own.

THINGS TO LOOK FOR

GENERAL

- a lot (not alot)
- all right (not alright)
- backup
- cannot (vs. can not)
- CD or CDs
- email (not e-mail)
- FAQ or FAQs
- flier
- HotSpot
- information about (not information on)
- Internet
- online
- snail mail
- voicemail
- Web site
- web address

MINISTRY-SPECIFIC

- All STARS
- Connection Café (with accented "e")
- GCCwired.com
- Heir Force Room
- Lifeline
- Next Step Resources
- Oasis
- Son City Kids
- WiredChurches.com (not Wired Churches)
- Wi-Fi™
- Monroe Circle Community Center (not MC3) – also called GCC's Community Center in downtown South Bend
- Manowê (Use with this tagline: GCC's retreat and conference center)
- Five Star
- Entermission, Inc.

VEHICLES & DELIVERY:

HOT	NOT
GCC logo	Ministry logos
Web site, enews, Bulletin	Ministry brochures
Event fact sheet	Event brochures
How can we take it to the next level?	What else can we add?
What does our guest need?	What's cool?
Less	More

VERBIAGE:

HOT	NOT
Connection	Intimacy
Group	Small Group
Community	Fellowship
Team	Committee
Program	Ministry (noun)
Serve	Ministry (verb)
Guest	Target Audience
Guest	Unchurched
Guest	Visitor
Volunteer Expo	Ministry Fair
Next Step	Go Deeper
Invite	Recruit
Opportunity	Need
Experience	Attend
Explore	Commit
Outreach	Missions
Reaching Out	
Growth	Maturity

WRITING FOR THE WEB

People read online content differently than they do print materials. The physical limitations of computer monitors, as well as the nature of a hypertext environment, prevent people from reading for long periods of time or in a linear fashion. While good writing is good writing, understanding these differences is crucial to communicating effectively on the Web.

Interestingly enough, in today's information age, people are becoming more accustomed to the reading style of web copy and are becoming more impatient with lengthy print copy. The transition has already begun to move to a "task-driven" reading approach as more and more documents are being published in scannable or bulleted formats. In other words, web copy translates well into printed material but print copy does not translate well into Web copy.

- "Chunk" text (break into bite-sized pieces) for quick and easy consumption.

- Use short phrases instead of full sentences to make a point.

- Be direct. Use active voice.

- Make one point per paragraph.

- Use a sans-serif font like Arial for easier readability on the Web.

- Avoid empty phrases, market-speak and floweriness. A reader is more likely to trust the content when it is not over-hyped.

- Eliminate vague modifiers (e.g., really, very, actually, sort of, etc.).

- Employ the "inverted pyramid" style of writing – place the main point of the topic in the first or second sentence instead of leading up to the topic sentence with introductory sentences.

- Break paragraph points into bulleted lists.

- Never use "click on" or "click here." Just make the subject a hyperlink.

  Example: **Register** now. (not "Click here to register.")
  Example: Connect at our special **events** or **small groups**. (not "Click here for small groups.")

<aside>253</aside>

APPLICATION

Right: We host Son City Kids at two locations:

- **Harbor Homes**
  Washington Street, South Bend, Indiana

- **Monroe Circle**
  Monroe Circle Community Center, South Bend, Indiana

Wrong: We host Son City Kids at two locations. You can choose the location that is most convenient for you. The first location is Harbor Homes on Washington Street in South Bend, IN. This was the first place we started meeting. We've been meeting there for approximately two years. The second location is in the Monroe Circle neighborhood.

EMPLOYEE HANDBOOK

A few sample pages of the one we created for Granger are included here, but you can download the full version from WiredChurches.com, edit it and make it your own.

INTRODUCTION

This handbook is designed to provide important information about working at Granger Community Church. Though we realize many of the policies and procedures within are quite boring, they are still important to communicate and we hope you find we've written them in such a way you won't fall asleep while reading.

While we've worked around the clock on this document, we have not been able to think of everything. And many of the things that did occur to us we chose not to include. Remember, we don't want you to fall asleep.

So, if you have questions not answered in this manual, don't be alarmed. Just ask your boss (if you don't know who that is, ask the person in the next cubicle) or the office administrator. We'll warn you in advance there are some things in this handbook we're encouraged by law to include. It's really hard to make those interesting, but we've done our best.

Have fun reading!

PAYDAY

Hooray, it's payday. Employees who desire to be paid are normally paid every two weeks on Fridays. (Aren't you glad it's not once a year?) Direct deposit is required. Pay is in U.S. dollars only. Sorry, no rupees, euros or monopoly money available.

Certain deductions from your paycheck may be for elective options, like insurance and 403(b) investments. Other deductions are required by law, like taxes.

The Administrative Council determines compensation packages for the Senior Pastor and the Executive Pastor. Compensation packages for all other staff are determined by the Senior Pastor and the Executive Pastor (in consultation with supervisors) and approved by the Administrative Council. All compensation packages are reviewed annually based on scope of the job description, performance and attitude.

Other changes in pay or benefits are based on a number of factors including overall budget, financial condition of the church, cost of living considerations, performance and value to the church. Normally, raises are not given until the beginning of the calendar year following the first entire year of employment (e.g., Waldo is hired in July 2008, he will probably not be considered for a raise until January 2010).

Hourly staff are required to record work hours on a weekly time sheet. Time-and-a-half will only be paid for hourly wage staff working in excess of 40 hours in a given week if those hours have been approved by their supervisor.

Shhh...Keep Your Lips Sealed

Compensation packages are personal and confidential. Employees should never discuss their compensation package with anyone, unless they are a member of your family. This is something we take very seriously. Sharing compensation information with others could cost you your job. It's that serious.

WEB SITE BEFORE

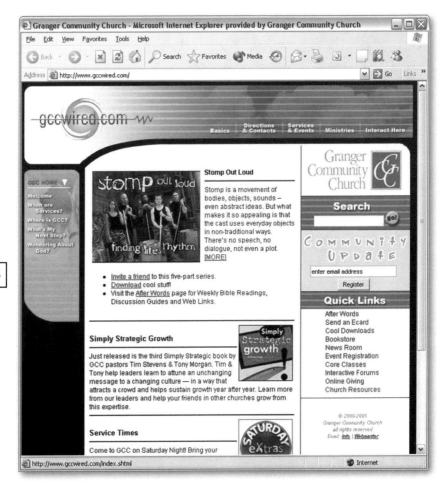

WEB SITE AFTER

BULLETIN BEFORE

8.5" x 17", folded, full color inside & outside

BULLETIN AFTER

Granger Community Church was founded by Mark and Sheila Beeson and has experienced 22 years of growth and changed lives. We have a passion to reflect God's truth through the arts; so music, drama and media are a big part of the way we communicate. We invest heavily in our children and students, believing them to be some of the greatest influencers of the church today.

Speaking of kids, our goal is to make this the best hour of your child's week and the most helpful hour of yours: To minimize distractions for adult guests and maximize your child's experience, we ask that children under seven participate in their age-appropriate classrooms.

The only thing we ask of you? It's simple: relax. No matter where you've been or what you've done, you matter to God. We're glad you're here. This service is our gift to you, no strings attached. If you're a guest today, please feel no obligation to give. If you're a Christ follower, we invite you to give joyfully.

One church . . . where you are. Our mission? Helping people take their next steps toward Christ . . . together. We have five identical services every weekend between two campuses: four in Granger and one in Elkhart at the Encore Cinemas on Cassopolis Street.

granger community church
Granger | Saturday at 5 & 7 p.m. Sunday at 9:30 & 11:30 a.m.
Elkhart | Sunday at 9:30 a.m.
630 E. University Dr. • Granger, IN 46530 • 574.243.3600 • GCCwired.com

Tell us about you.

Granger Campus
Saturday: O 5 p.m. O 7 p.m.
Sunday: O 9:30 a.m. O 11:30 a.m.

Elkhart Campus
Sunday: O 9:30 a.m.

Name		Birthday	/	/
Spouse		Birthday	/	/
Address	City	State	ZIP	
Phone		OH OW OC		

Email
O Yes, send me the weekly enewsletter.

Weekend Experience

Five identical services, two campuses.
WEEKEND | Help Wanted: I've Never Seen It This Bad. January 17-18

Own Your Journey

Groups. Monday night is group night, 6:30-8 p.m.
- **View Point** (Bible study), launches January 19 (six weeks)
- **Turning Point** (personal life change), launches January 26 (ten weeks)
- **Starting Point for Married** (friendship), launches February 9 (six weeks)
- **Financial Peace University**, launches February 23 (13 weeks)
RSVP and get started at GCCwired.com or Guest Services.

Arts Volunteer Expo. Tuesday, February 24, 7-8:30 p.m. at the Granger Campus. If you enjoy running audio or video equipment, operating cameras, creating media, photography, graphic design or are a vocalist, a musician or actor, learn more about opportunities to use your skills on the arts teams at the Granger and Elkhart Campuses.

Second Saturday. Saturday, February 14, 8:30 a.m.-12 p.m. Choose from a variety of serving options, from helping underprivileged children to feeding the hungry. Pick your location.
- Meet at the Granger Campus.
- Elkhart Campus, meet at the Encore Cinemas in Elkhart.
- Marshall County, meet in Plymouth at the Plymouth Hospital Meeting Room.

Beyond I Do. Ready to take your next step into a great marriage? Learn how to secure your future marriage at this seminar for engaged couples. Saturday, February 28, 8 a.m.-4:30 p.m. Cost: $60 per couple.

Also Happening @ Elkhart

Connection Point. If you're new to the Elkhart Campus, spend an evening sharing stories and getting to know Campus Pastor Jeff Bell and his wife Leslee. Sunday, January 25, 6-7:30 p.m. RSVP to get started.

Next

NEXT WEEKEND
Help Wanted | I Think We Might Lose Everything, January 24-25
Granger: Saturday at 5 & 7 p.m. Sunday at 9:30 & 11:30 a.m.
Elkhart: Sunday at 9:30 a.m.

MIDWEEK | Meets at the Granger Campus.
- **January Journey Bible Classes.** January 21, 26 at 6:30 p.m.
  2 Timothy | Spiritual Practices: Friendship | Financial Fights, Fear & Faith
- **1st Wednesday.** February 4, 6:30 p.m. Monthly worship and Communion celebration.

Students (GSM) | Meets at the Granger Campus.
Middle School (6-8th grade): Sundays, 4-5 p.m.
High School (9-12th grade): Sundays, 7-8 p.m.
Come early and stay late. Hang out a half hour before and after.

- **Middle School Girlz Only.** Friday, January 23, 6:30-9 p.m. Go snow tubing with your friends at George Wilson Park. Cost: $5.
- **High School Chick Nite.** Friday, January 30, 6-10 p.m. Go ice skating with the girls at Merrifield Ice Skating Rink. Cost: $5.
- **GSM Parents Group** launches February 8.

MERGE | Meets at the Granger Campus. 18-25? Get connected. Wednesdays at 6:15 p.m. in the Great Room.

About my experience today:
_____
_____
_____

You can pray for me about:
_____
_____
_____

Prayer needs will be shared with the pastors, staff and volunteers on the GCC prayer team.

8.5" x 5.5", folded, full color outside, black and white inside

ENEWS BEFORE

ENEWS AFTER

MINISTRY FAIR HANDOUT
BEFORE

...AND HERE.

You can make a difference, across town or the other side of the globe. It starts here. There are dozens of areas to serve... **to make a difference.**

Representatives from each of the following areas will be available these weekends to answer questions, share information and help you take an immediate next step to get involved.

★ September 13/14 ★ Saturdays 4:30 - 5 p.m. & 6-8:30 p.m.
★ September 20/21 ★ Sundays 8:15 a.m. - 1:30 p.m.
★ October 11/12

ALL STARS (Infant - 5th Grade)
* Classroom Interaction -
  teachers, leaders, small group facilitators
* Creative Arts - lead worship, prepare creative elements
* Administrative Support -
  registration, weekday preparation, data entry

OASIS (6th - 8th Grade)
* Relational Interaction - Oasis (weekly gathering)
  leaders and team members, small group facilitators
* Creative & Technical Arts -
  drama, band, video, photographer, audio, media, lighting
* Support - childcare, administrative assistance

LIFELINE (9th - 12th Grade)
* Relational Interaction -
  weekly gathering of leaders and team members
* Creative & Technical Arts -
  drama, video, media, photographer, lighting
* Support - childcare, administrative assistance

COUPLES CONNECTIONS
* Marriage Enrichment -
  plan events to help couples take steps in their marriage
* Home Group Leaders - facilitate relational groups,
  help develop systems... get connected with other couples.

MEN CONNECTIONS
* Sports - help plan, promote, facilitate sporting opportunities -
  or play!
* Retreats - assist in planning, leading and connecting men

...AND HERE.

SINGLES CONNECTIONS
* Connection Events - regularly scheduled gatherings designed
  around interest and life-stage
* Retreats - new opportunity to connect and encourage
* Home Groups - facilitate or visit weekly gatherings.

WOMEN CONNECTIONS
* Tuesday Morning Soul Food -a weekly gathering to connect and grow
* Retreats - assist in planning, leading and organizing annual events
  to connect women
* Home Groups - facilitate, organize, promote
* Community Involvement - participate, plan, lead projects that
  serve needs in the Michiana area

NEW BEGINNINGS
* Home Groups - facilitate 4-week group, discovering the Bible,
  prayer and essentials of personal relationship with God
* Innovate Connection Processes - assist in connecting new
  believers, developing strategies for initial next steps

FIRST IMPRESSIONS
* Relational Interaction/Experience Creators - greeters, hospitality
  team, medical services, security, shuttle drivers, traffic team
* Behind-the-Scenes Support - Bulletin assembly, refreshment
  team, administrative support

NEXT STEP RESOURCES
* Bookstore -customer service, scheduling, shipping/receiving,
  weekday assistance
* Connection Café - assist guests, product runners,
  food buyers/ordering, scheduling
* Media Duplication - help duplicate tapes and CDs of weekend,
  New Community and training messages

SHAPE RESOURCES
* Consultants - assist members in finding serving opportunities that
  match their SHAPE
* Ministry Liaisons - assist ministry leaders by representing
  specific areas and linking new and potential team members

CAMPUS OPERATIONS
* Building - housekeeping / facility services, event set-up
  and turnover, facility maintenance, aquarium care,
  department of the interior
* Grounds - green thumb, birds of a feather, spring and fall
  campus work days, winter grounds, vehicle maintenance

VOLUNTEER EXPO HANDOUT
AFTER

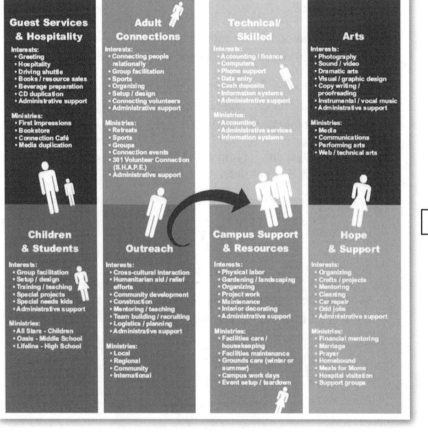

TYPICAL BULLETIN ANNOUNCEMENT
BEFORE

Beyond I Do

Pre-marital workshop for couples who are to be engaged. Would Like to include note that both parties need to attend.

Would like them registered individually. Would like 3 questions "Name of fiance" and "wedding date" "will your ceremony be performed at GCC?"

Two Saturdays, July 11 and July 18, 2009. 8:00 am-1 PM. Cost is $30 per person.

AFTER

Beyond I Do. Ready to take your next step into a great marriage? Learn how to secure your future relationship at this seminar for engaged couples. Part 1: Saturday, July 11, 8 a.m.-1 p.m. Part 2: July 18, 8 a.m.-1 p.m. Cost: $60 per couple.

FREE MARKET RESEARCH

- bea.gov

- claritas.com/MyBestSegments/Default.jsp

- census.gov*

- milkeninstitute.org

- corporateinformation.com

- knowthis.com

- censusscope.org

- churchrelevance.com/category/research

- Easy Analytic Software, Inc.

- easidemographics.com/cgi-bin/login_free.asp

- freedemographics.com

- melissadata.com/Lookups/index.htm

- U.S. Census Bureau sites

- factfinder.census.gov/home/saff/main.html?_lang=en

- census.gov/epcd/www/zipstats.html*

- zipskinny.com

* Don't forget to add the www first.

EVOLUTION OF A CENTRALIZED COMMUNICATIONS DEPARTMENT

We didn't get there overnight. Here's our story, told in average weekend attendance increments.

1,000

- No dedicated communications staff.

- Centralized calendar and church budget.

- Decentralized marketing efforts and promotional dollars for individual ministries.

- Each ministry did their own marketing, Web site, brochures, fulfillment, mailings, lobbied for platform announcements, etc.

- Volunteer built first Web site. Next generation was built by a web company and maintained by admin services pastor and help desk guy.

- Our senior pastor's administrative assistant handled the bulletin and series promotion.

- We used a hired freelance designer to design series promotion.

3,500

- Web director hired part time (Kem) but turned into communications director instead. Spent two years developing processes and systems for information flow before focusing on Web site.

- At the same time, a communications intern and part-time communications manager (Jami) came on staff to help implement the processes, start the weekly enews, centralize marketing efforts, build volunteer teams for graphics, writing, etc.

- Started out at "proofers/reviewers" of ministry marketing efforts.

4,000

- Made reallocation of church budgeting resources to invest in a revamped Web site.

5,000

- Communications team expanded. Kem and Jami became full-time.

- Hired communications coordinator, web services coordinator, web director and back office specialist.

- Team is now central support for all marketing efforts. Works as consultants to various ministries.

THE EVOLUTION OF A SUPERTEAM

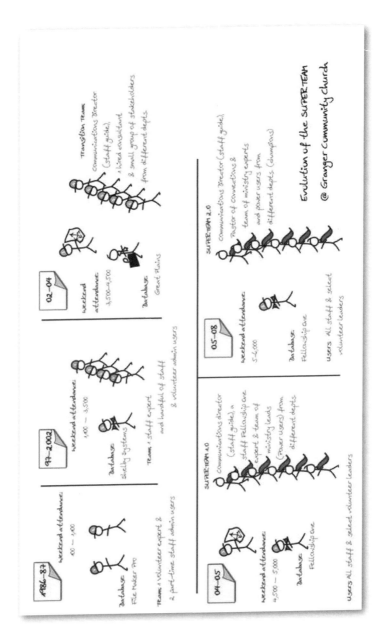

INSPIRATION

Are People Letting You In or Shutting You Out?

- Stay alert. This is hazardous work I'm assigning you. You're going to be like sheep running through a wolf pack, so don't call attention to yourselves. Be as cunning as a snake, inoffensive as a dove. (Matthew 10:16, Message)

- Their heads were spinning; they couldn't make head or tail of any of it. They talked back and forth, confused: "What's going on here?" (Acts 2:12, Message)

- The assembly was in confusion: Some were shouting one thing, some another. Most people didn't even know why they were there. (Acts 19:32, NIV)

- The god of this age has blinded the minds of unbelievers, so that they cannot see the light of the gospel of the glory of Christ, who is the image of God. (2 Corinthians 4:4, NIV)

- Now that we know what we have—Jesus, this great High Priest with ready access to God—let's not let it slip through our fingers. We don't have a priest who is out of touch with our reality. He's been through weakness and testing, experienced it all—all but the sin. So let's walk right up to him and get what he is so ready to give. Take the mercy, accept the help. (Hebrews 4:15-16, Message)

Best Practices Make a Difference.

- Then the master told his servant, Go out to the roads and country lanes and compel them to come in, so that my house will be full. (Luke 14:23, TNIV)

- The teaching of your word gives light, so even the simple can understand. (Psalm 119:130, NLT)

- Cut to the quick, those who were there listening asked Peter and the other apostles, "Brothers! Brothers! So now what do we do?" (Acts 2:37, Message)

- Now go, write it on a tablet before them and inscribe it on a scroll, that it may serve in the time to come as a witness forever. (Isaiah 30:8, NASB)

The Responsibility of Getting Buy-in.

- Understand this, my dear brothers and sisters: You must all be quick to listen, slow to speak, and slow to get angry. (James 1:19, NLT)

- And those who believed met together and shared everything they had. (Acts 2:44, NLT)

- I beg you in the name of the Lord Jesus Christ to stop arguing among yourselves. Let there be real harmony among you so that there won't be splits in the church. Be of one mind, united in thought and purpose. (1 Corinthians 1:10, NLT)

- Everyone around was in awe—all those wonders and signs done through the apostles! And all the believers lived in a wonderful harmony, holding everything in common. They sold whatever they owned and pooled their resources so that each person's need was met. (Acts 2: 43-45, Message)

- A huge cloud of witnesses is all around us. So let us throw off everything that stands in our way. Let us throw off any sin that holds on to us so tightly. Let us keep on running the race marked out for us. (Hebrews 12: 1, NIRV)

If you enjoyed this book and are looking for more like it, check out...

Find these and other high-impact resources in your favorite formats at WiredChurches.com, like downloadable videos, message MP3s, graphics, small group study guides, administrative forms and more.

GIVING CREDIT WHERE CREDIT IS DUE

This was the hardest part of the book for me to write. I literally put it off until the last possible minute. Have you ever heard *"we is smarter than me?"* Well, it's more true than ever in the case of this project. It's just impossible to find words that do my gratitude and appreciation justice. To the scores of people who listened, inspired, encouraged, motivated, guided, assisted and challenged—here goes my best attempt at an impossible task.

- **Jesus.** Thank you for loving me when I was (and still am) unlovable and for showing me how to love others.

- **Investors.** Thank you Mom, Dad, Leanna Vite, Mark Meyer, Tony Morgan and Tim Stevens for seeing beyond the exterior to find the potential inside of me. You pulled me out of mediocre comfort zones and quite literally saved my life.

- **Cheerleaders.** At home and the office, gobs and gobs of love and thanks go to Erin, Emmi, Easton, Mel, and Bunny Meyer as well as Jami Ruth, Lisa DeSelm, Daryl McMullen, Jason Powell, Jeanna Miller, Ed Buford, Matt Metzger and Justin Moore for your unconditional support, sacrifice and stamina through the writing. You carried my load and your own (and refused to allow me to carry guilt for it). Morning, noon and night you endured my craziness through the highs and lows to see this project through.

- **Leaders.** My gratitude, reverance and loyalty goes to my pastor, Mark Beeson and the rest of the senior management team at Granger Community Church. You have shaped me, supported me and changed my DNA.

- **Contributors.** I owe a debt of gratitude to Tad Long, Janet Schwind and George Watkins. You turned a manuscrap into a manuscript (you made it all better). Also, thank you Chad Allen and Jessica Kelley. Without your coaching and personal investment, I never would have got my head around a plan in the first place.

- **Reviewers.** For your selfless participation and input, all praise and recognition goes to Jim Henry, Blake Atwood, Blake Thompson, Renee Bleich, Jeremy Scheller, Shari Wolfgang, Melisa Johnson, Tim Schraeder, Zach Montroy, Jeff Christian, Shawn Wood, Brent Hodge, Steve Denny, Joel DeSelm, Phil Cooke, Amber Cox, Dustin Hannifin, Pat Kase, Michelle Wegner, Matt Kerner, Karl King, Karen Gadson, Bill Robinson, Melanie Rosander, Lindsay Wasik (Helman), Steve Smith and countless other blog, Facebook and Twitter friends. Special thanks to Faye Bryant, Jessica Mast, Sam Mahlstadt and John Ireland for responding to my last minute proofing SOS. You rescued me.

- **Environment.** For someone like me to write a book, it takes the perfect balance of minimal distractions and constant variety. Color me impossible. But, there are a few people that actually helped to create the perfectly impossible conditions for me to perservere. Thank you, Kyle Sagarsee for the campus wi-fi pass. Thank you, creators of Twitter and Facebook for saving me from depressing boredom and isolation. Thank you, Michiana restaurants, for feeding me and my family for six months. Thank you, Battlestar Galactica, John Adams and The Dark Knight for amazing background soundtracks.

- **Inspiration.** Finally, a shout out to all the professionals and organizations who inspired me, provided examples and graciously allowed me to mention and learn from them along the way. For being generous sports, thanks to the Granger Community Church staff team, Brad Abare, Aspire!One, Chris Forbes, Walt Disney, Seth Godin, Guy Kawasaki, Andy Sernovitz, 37 Signals, Xplane, Lego, Google, Unum, PepsiOne, Moe's, and Starbucks (among many others).

Whew, that was not easy. I'll end this with a humble heart.

ENDNOTES

Chapter 1

1. PepsiCo. Inc., http://www.oneify.com.

2. http://flickr.com/photos/70411511@N00/72753726.

3. David Armano, "It's the Conversation Economy, Stupid," BusinessWeek.com, April 9, 2007, http://www.businessweek.com/innovate/content/apr2007/id20070409_372598. htm?chan=innovation_innovation+%2B+design_insight.

4. Nelson Books, New Rebellion Handbook: A Holy Uprising Making Real the Extraordinary in Everyday Life (Nashville, TN: Thomas Nelson, Inc., 2006).

5. Lego.com, http://www.lego.com/en-US/default.aspx?domainredir=lego.com.

Chapter 2

1. Richard Saul Wurman, Information Anxiety (New York: Doubleday, 1989, 32).

2. "WWW Faqs: How Many Websites Are There?" Boutell.com, Inc., February 15, 2007, http://www.boutell.com/newfaq/misc/sizeofweb.html.

3. "Mail Carriers Fired for not Delivering Bulk Mail," St. Petersburg Times, November 12, 2005.

4. ThinkSimpleNow, "How to Reduce Information Overload," http://thinksimplenow. com/productivity/how-to-reduce-information-overload/.

5. Bill Breen, "Marketing: Breaking through the Noise (Fast Company)," Robert Paterson's Radio Weblog, February, 2003, http://radio.weblogs.com/0107127/stories/2003/02/01/marketingBreakingThroughTheNoisefastCompany.html

6. Katya Andresen, "Your 'New' Is not News," Katya's Non-Profit Marketing Blog: Getting to the Point, August 30, 2007, http://nonprofitmarketingblog.com.

7. Mediaedge:cia Research (paper presented at the Word Of Mouth Marketing Summit, Chicago, Illinois, March 29–30, 2005).

8. Yankelovich Research (paper presented at the Word Of Mouth Marketing Summit, Chicago, Illinois, March 29–30, 2005).

9. Jim Nail, Forrester Research, "Consumer Respect, Consumer Control, Consumer Trust and Marketers Learning to Live With It" (presented at the Word Of Mouth Marketing Summit, Chicago, Illinois, March 29–30, 2005).

10. Phil Cooke, Branding Faith: Why Some Churches and Nonprofits Impact Culture and Others Don't (Ventura, CA: Regal, 2008).

Chapter 3

1. Note to CMO. http://note-to-cmo.blogspot.com/2007/10/note-to-cmo-starbucks-is-justlike-you.html.

2. Rusty Weston, "Careers: Work among True Believers?" Fast Company, October 10, 2007, http://fastcompany.com/blog/rusty-weston/job-world/careers-work-among-true-believers.

3. Mediaedge:cia Research (paper presented at the Word Of Mouth Marketing Summit, Chicago, Illinois, March 29–30, 2005).

4. Jessica Hagy, "A Friend Told Me about It," Indexed, September 9, 2008, http://thisisindexed.com/2008/09/page/2/.

Chapter 4

1. David Armano, "It's the Conversation Economy, Stupid," Business Week, April 9, 2007, http://businessweek.com/innovate/content/apr2007/id20070409_372598.htm?chan=innovation_innovation+%2B+design_insight.

2. Marshal McLuhan & Lewis H. Lapham, Understanding Media: The Extension of Man (Cambridge, MA: The MIT Press, 1964).

3. Katya Andresen, "What to Do About That New Generation," Katya's Non-Profit Marketing Blog: Getting to the Point, August 21, 2007, http://www.nonprofitmarketingblog.com/comments/what_to_do_about_that_new_generation/.

4. BBC News, "Turning into Digital Goldfish," February 22, 2002, http://news.bbc.co.uk/2/hi/science/nature/1834682.stm.

5. Josh Catone, "What the Heck Happened to Our Attention Spans," July 25, 2008, Sitepoint, http://sitepoint.com/blogs/2008/07/25/what-the-heck-happened-to-our-attention-spans/.

6. WIRED, "Mobile Device Culture," March 2008.

7. Kelley Hartnett, "Rela-tech-ship," Blue Is a Circle, September 30, 2008, http://blueisacircle.blogspot.com/2008/09/rela-tech-ship.html.

Chapter 5

1. Chris Forbes, "The One Simple Secret that Will Help You Reach More People," ministry marketing coach.com, December 27, 2006, http://ministrymarketingcoach.com/blog/2006/12/27/the-one-simple-secret-that-will-help-you-reach-more-people/.

2. 1 Corinthians 9:24–26; Hebrews 12:1–2.

Chapter 6

1. Robert K. Cooper, Get Out of Your Own Way (New York: Crown Business, 2006).

2. Nancy Hoft Consulting, http://world-ready.com/.

3. Gary Ferraro, Cultural Dimension of International Business, 5th ed. (Upper Saddle River, NJ: Prentice Hall, 2005).

4. Richard L. Reising, Beyond Relevance. http://www.beyondrelevance.com/.

5. Relevant Magazine, March, 2008.

6. Mark L. Waltz, Lasting Impressions (Loveland, CO: Group Publishing, Inc., 2008).

7. Disney Institute, Be Our Guest (New York: Disney Editions, 2001).

Chapter 7

1. http://moderntoilet.com (no longer active).

2. Image found at http://yeinjee.com/asianpop/wp-content/uploads/2007/11/taiwanese-modern-toilet-02.jpg.

3. Matt Lindeman, "[On Writing] Marketing Madlibs," 37signals, February 4, 2008, http://37signals.com/svn/posts/814-on-writing-marketing-madlibs.

4. Marty Sklar in Disney Institute, Be Our Guest (New York: Disney Editions, 2001).

Chapter 8

1. Michelle Wegner, "When Schools Go Green Update," Michelle Wegner, August 21, 2008, http://michellewegner.typepad.com/my_weblog/2008/08/when-schools-go-green-update.html.

2. Tim Schraeder, "Communications Revolution Part 3: The Death of the Weekly Program/Bulletin/Newsletter," Tim Schraeder.com, July 31, 2008, http://timschraeder.typepad.com/cr8ve/2008/07/communications-revolution-part-3-the-death-of-the-weekly-programbulletinnewsletter.html.

3. 37signals, LLC, Getting Real (Chicago: 37signals, LLC, 2006) https://gettingreal.37signals.com/ch01_What_is_Getting_Real.php.

4. Eric Kintz, "Why Blog Post Frequency Does Not Matter Anymore," Marketing Profs Daily Fix, June 6, 2006, http://mpdailyfix.com/2006/06/w_why_blog_post_frequency_does.html.

Chapter 9

1. John B. Priestley, Thoughts in the Wilderness (New York: Harper and Bros., 1957).

2. Image found at http://www.bestlife.co.za/uploads/images/par_img_7_52.jpg.

3. Jeremy Scheller, "3 Easy Ways to Lose Your Identity," JeremyScheller.com, February 20, 2008, http://jeremyscheller.com/2008/02/20/3-easy-ways-to-lose-your-identity/.

4. Andy Sernovitz, Word of Mouth Marketing: How Smart Companies Get People Talking (Chicago: Kaplan Publishing, 2006).

5. Mark Batterson, "The Art of Reframing," Evotional.com, October 23, 2006, http://www.evotional.com/2006/10/art-of-reframing.html.

Chapter 10

1. Steve Smith, "Don't Complicate the Solution," orderedlist.com, November 14, 2007, http://orderedlist.com/articles/don-t-complicate-the-solution.

2. Ibid.

3. Tony Morgan, "10 Easy Ways to Keep Me from Visiting Your Church Because I Visited Your Website," Tonymorganlive.com, May 14, 2005, tonymorganlive.com/2005/05/14/10-easy-ways-to-keep-me-from-visiting-your-church-because-i-visited-your-website.

Chapter 11

1. lbert Hubbard, "Elbert Hubbard Quotes," The Quotations Page, http://www.quotationspage.com/quotes/Elbert_Hubbard/.

2. Daniel Pink, A Whole New Mind: Why Right-Brainers Will Rule the Future, (New York: The Berkley Publishing Group, 2005).

Chapter 12

1. Marcia Conner, "The Seeing/Believing Gap," Fast Company, February 2006, http://fastcompany.com/resources/learning/conner/the-seeingbelieving-gap-092807.html.

2. This Is Broken, http://www.goodexperience.com/tib/archives/2005/12/for_fun_mt_st_h.html.

3. How to Change the World, http://blog.guykawasaki.com/2006/02/the_art_of_rain.html.

Chapter 13

1.   Change This, http://changethis.com/48.01.CorporateChange.

2.   Ibid.

Chapter 14

1.   Project Annihilation, http://www.engadget.com/2005/03/24/ project-annihilation-death-of-an-itrip/.

2.   Wikipedia, s.v. "Peter Drucker," http://en.wikipedia.org/wiki/Peter_Drucker.

Chapter 15

1.   More about Christine Caine at http://www.equipandempower.org/about. asp?inttype=5.

MY NOTES